Living in the
NAMES OF GOD
Bible Study

HIS MAJESTY AND YOU

Judy Squier

JUDY ❧ SQUIER

www.judysquier.com

Self-published by Judy Squier.
(www.judysquier.com)

Cover & interior design by Naphtalie Joiner (www.scatterjoydesigns.com)
Cover photo & author photo by Naphtalie Joiner (www.scatterjoyphotos.com)

Names of God artwork by Mia Moreing Russell (www.miarussellartist.com)
Each picture is copyrighted by the artist.

Scripture quotations marked AMP are taken from *The Amplified Bible*. Copyright © 1965, 1987 by The Zondervan Corporation. *The Amplified New Testament* Copyright © 1958, 1987 by The Lockman Foundation. Used by permission.

Scripture quotations marked KJV are taken from the *King James Version* of the Bible. Public domain.

Scripture quotations marked MSG are from *The Message*. Copyright © by Eugene H. Peterson 1993, 1994, 1995, 1996, 2000, 2001, 2002. Used by permission of NavPress Publishing Group.

Scripture quotations marked NASB are taken from the *New American Standard Bible®*, Copyright © 1960, 1962, 1963, 1968, 1971, 1972, 1973, 1975, 1977, 1995 by the Lockman Foundation. Used by permission. (www.Lockman.org)

Scripture quotations marked NIV are taken from *The Holy Bible, New International Version®*, *(NIV)* Copyright © 1973, 1978, 1984, 2011 by Biblica, Inc.® Used by permission. All rights reserved worldwide.

Scripture quotations marked NLT are taken from the *Holy Bible, New Living Translation*, Copyright © 1996, 2004, 2007. Used by permission of Tyndale House Publishers, Inc., Wheaton, Illinois 60189, U.S.A. All rights reserved.

Scripture quotations marked TLB are taken from *The Living Bible*. Copyright © 1971. Used by permission of Tyndale House Publishers, Inc., Carol Stream, Illinois, 60188. All rights reserved.

Disclaimer: At the onset may I beg your scholastic mercy. These bible studies are not intended for microscopic examination by Hebrew scholars, but they are intended to facilitate an attainable-to-all relationship with Jehovah God whose grandeur requires oh so many names.

Squier, Judy
Living in the Names of God Bible Study / by Judy Squier
      ISBN-10: 1497376181
      ISBN-13: 978-1497376182

Printed in the United States of America

❤ ❤ ❤

DEDICATED TO MY THREE DAUGHTERS –
Emily Beth, Elizabeth Christine and Naphtalie Joy
May God's names become the love of your lives.
May you grow old in grace, emulating your father,
whose worship continues nightly as he sleeps.
Music to my ears is his intermittent:
Thank You, Lord,
Thank You, Lord,
Thank You, Lord.

Contents

In Appreciation

Heartfelt Thanks:

To *Elohim, El Elyon, Jehovah, Jehovah Raah, Jehovah Shammah, El Roi, Jehovah Nissi, Jehovah Tsidkenu, El Shaddai, El Gibbor, Jehovah Jireh, Adonai, Adonai Tsuri, Jehovah Rapha, Jehovah Shalom, Jehovah Mekoddishkem, El Olam* and *Go'el* –
I'll praise your names, Lord, into eternity!

To Amy, my editor extraordinaire, for her in-depth content edit that elevated these studies to a new level of excellence.

To Mia, my names of God artist, whose creative art expands our God-worship to new heights.

To Naphy, my graphic designer/photographer daughter, who for the third time has carried her mom's material across the finish line to publication.

To Ginny, whose confidence moved the material in this Bible study from my heart to a roomful of women eager to broaden their understanding of God and His names.

To Joanie, one of the women attending the Bible study who insisted, "Judy, this material has to be published!"

To Alma, a seeker of Truth who, while attending the Bible study, found Jesus to be the Lover of her soul.

To Cousin Sue and Bill & Edie Miller, forever prayer warriors, who have faithfully prayed three books into existence.

To Pastors Bob Bonner, Don Needham and Dean Smith, for sharing their theological knowledge and love of the Hebrew names of God.

i

PREFACE

The term "God" is possibly the most generic word on the planet. As the universal expression for every religion's concept of a supernatural higher power, it is often defined through the "eye of the beholder."

As followers of Christ, the title "God" is usually the starting point as we grapple with concepts of origins, purpose, hope, faith, values and eternity. But even in a faith system that values a personal relationship with a Living Being, God can seem to be a distant, inaccessible, unknowable, impersonal cosmic force.

For me, God was that powerful yet unknown abstraction until I began to study His names and their meanings. Finding that God is identified in Scripture through dozens of personal names, titles and descriptions has been one of my greatest epiphanies! Some of these names were given through God's revelation; others were given by those who witnessed His actions.

God takes on an entirely new dimension as we begin to learn and drill down into His names. He becomes more than a religious crutch when we trust Him as Provider. We understand His tenderness when we experience Him as Shepherd. Salvation by grace – and grace alone – is conceivable when we know Him as our Righteousness. Contentment and peace are realities when we find Him as *Shalom*. There are incredible riches to be mined when we leave the surface designation of "God" and begin to ponder the width – and plumb the depths – of names like *El Shaddai, Jehovah Nissi* or *El Elyon*.

I proclaim this from experience – not theory. My own journey with exploring and applying His Names intensified on September 11, 2012 upon hearing the doctor's words, "You have cancer." As a pastor, I am familiar with the "usual passages" we read and quote to give encouragement, peace and consolation. Those Scriptures were my first stops. But then I went to The Names! Keeping a journal of what I called GOD MARKERS, it was amazing how often I found exactly the words I needed to get through a head shave, chemo drip, C-scan or radiation treatment. As of this writing, I am in remission but have been told I will never be free of the disease. Knowing a medical diagnosis has the power to again "rattle my world" keeps me on a quest to grow in intimacy with, and knowledge of, my Redeemer God.

My challenge to you is to become radically familiar with The Names. This wonderful study by Judy will likely take you to depths of understanding – and heights of exaltation – you haven't yet experienced!

Pastor Don Needham
Woodmen Valley Chapel
Winter 2014

יהוה יהוה יהוה יהוה יהוה יהוה יהוה יהוה יהוה יהוה

Our help is in the name of the LORD.

Psalm 124:8a (NASB)

ELOHIM
Mighty Creator

EL GIBBOR
Mighty Warrior

EL ELYON
The Most High God

JEHOVAH JIREH
The LORD Will Provide

JEHOVAH
I AM WHO I AM

ADONAI
Lord and Master

JEHOVAH RAAH
The LORD My Shepherd

ADONAI TSURI
The Lord My Rock

The Names of God
REFERENCE GUIDE

JEHOVAH SHAMMAH
The LORD is There

JEHOVAH RAPHA
The LORD Who Heals

EL ROI
The God Who Sees

JEHOVAH SHALOM
The LORD is Peace

JEHOVAH NISSI
The LORD is My Banner

JEHOVAH MEKODDISH-KEM
The LORD Who Sanctifies

JEHOVAH TSIDKENU
The LORD Our Righteous-ness

EL OLAM
The Everlasting God

EL SHADDAI
The All-Sufficient God

GO'EL
God My Redeemer

Psalm 124:8a (NASB)

Our help is in the name of the LORD.

יהוה יהוה יהוה יהוה יהוה יהוה יהוה יהוה יהוה יהוה

vii

SCRIPTURE GUIDE
First Appearance of Each Name

*"Your name, God,
evokes a train of Hallelujahs
wherever it is spoken,
near and far."*

Psalm 48:10 MSG

1

His Majesty and You

LIVING IN THE NAMES OF GOD

INTRODUCTION

Is it possible to know God on a first-name basis? Does the God who created the universe really care about me? Could it be true that He loves me even on bad days when I can't love myself?

God resounds "Yes" to the above questions. More than anything He desires a relationship with us. He desires that we know and love Him as He knows and loves us. He desires to be intimately involved in our lives. He didn't create us only to then say, "Now leave Me alone and figure out the rest on your own."

Pastor Bob Bonner, in his series Facing Life's Demands, says:

> God did not just create you and initiate a relationship with you so then to leave you to your own devices to figure out life. He wants to build a relationship with you whereby you can experience Him throughout your day and in every good activity and troubling time you may face. He wants you to know Him and the reality of His presence in your life more than

you want it! Furthermore, when you come to Him, through trusting Jesus Christ as your Lord and Savior, He is going to make sure you get to that point. It may be through His loving discipline or through the school of hard knocks, but love never quits. He wants a relationship with you.[1]

WHY STUDY THE NAMES OF GOD?

Knowing God's names will help you recognize Him in your everyday experiences. Soon you may catch yourself saying things like:

- *Elohim*, thank You, for that creative idea.
- Bless You, *Jehovah Jireh*, for providing what I needed.
- I praise You, *Jehovah Shalom*, for Your calm as my life spins out of control.

Knowing Him by name gives you the Right Person to thank for the blessings and to trust in the trials.

To know Him is to love Him. And to know Him is to better understand His love for you. Ultimately, knowing He loves you helps you to come to the place where you can say: "I am lovable."

Knowing Him gives you permission to admit your powerlessness because He promises His power: "Whatever you need, I AM."

God Created Us for Coram Deo

When asked, "What's the big idea of the Christian life?" theologian R.C. Sproul's response was,

> *Coram Deo* captures the essence of the Christian life. This phrase literally refers to something that takes place in the presence of or before the face of God. To live *coram Deo* is to live one's entire life in the presence of God. . . .

> To live in the presence of God is to understand that whatever we are doing and wherever we are doing it, we are acting under the gaze of God. There is no place so remote that we can escape His penetrating gaze.[2]

What about you? How often do you think about God or sense His presence? Constantly? Several times a day? Once a week? Religious holidays? Rarely? Never?

The Secret: Life in Relationship with God

Psalm 46 makes known the relationship God longs to have with each one of us. He longs for us to run to Him when life is a pressure cooker, when we are in over our heads, when our nerves are frayed and fried.

1. Read Psalm 46. According to verse 1, what does God want to be for us?

2. When God becomes that for you, what can you then say (verse 2a)?

3. Verses 2 and 3 describe extreme natural disasters. Sometimes our personal daily disasters feel as big or bigger. List three of your current disasters.

4. Sometimes just the fear of disaster can take us down. List several of your biggest fears.

5. God offers a solution when fear pins us to the mat. His solution includes an action on our part plus a foundational belief so that He can do His part. Read Psalm 46:10. What are we commanded to do? _____ and

_____.

6. Psalm 46:10 is the heartbeat of the *Living in the Names of God* study. In the New International Version (NIV) the verse says, *"Be still and know that I am God"*; the New American Standard Bible (NASB) reads, *"Cease striving and know that I am God."* We are either striving to make life work apart from

God *or* our knowledge of His character enables us to allow Him to be in control of our lives. It's one or the other; it can't be both. As the popular saying goes, "Know God and know peace, or no God and no peace."

- Give a specific example of knowing God and knowing peace in your life.

- Give an example of no God and no peace in your life.

- Personalize the verse a little more and share how you have succeeded and failed in its application this week.

7. As you learn to know God by His names through these lessons, you will be better able to allow Him to become your *refuge and strength* (no matter what the test). Practicing His presence will strengthen the habit of *being still and knowing He is God*. Striving will end when you truly believe this truth: It doesn't depend on me!

- What or who are you holding on to that is keeping you from God's refuge and strength?

- Are you willing to hand that over to God as an act of worship? How will you do that right now?

EIGHTEEN NAMES OF GOD

This study includes eighteen Hebrew names of God (there are many more) that have met me at various points of need. These names continue to help me understand:

- Who He is
- Who He wants to be in our lives
- Who we are
- Who we can become in relationship with Him

Each name represents a way God wants us to know Him.

1. *Elohim* – Mighty Creator
2. *El Elyon* – The Most High God
3. *Jehovah* – I AM WHO I AM
4. *Jehovah Raah* – The LORD My Shepherd
5. *Jehovah Shammah* – The LORD is There
6. *El Roi* – The God Who Sees
7. *Jehovah Nissi* – The LORD is My Banner
8. *Jehovah Tsidkenu* – The LORD Our Righteousness
9. *El Shaddai* – The All-Sufficient God
10. *El Gibbor* – Mighty Warrior
11. *Jehovah Jireh* – The LORD Will Provide
12. *Adonai* – Lord and Master
13. *Adonai Tsuri* – The Lord My Rock
14. *Jehovah Rapha* – The LORD Who Heals
15. *Jehovah Shalom* – The LORD is Peace
16. *Jehovah Mekoddishkem* – The LORD Who Sanctifies
17. *El Olam* – The Everlasting God
18. *Go'el* – God My Redeemer

In this *Living in the Names of God Bible Study*, we will explore these Hebrew names of God found in the Old Testament. Each lesson will contain a name with its meaning, a discussion of where it appears in the Bible and an opportunity to explore what that name means to you personally.

LIFE'S GREATEST GOAL

In his book *Knowing God*, J.I. Packer conveys the importance of our knowing God, through the following questions and answers:

- *What were we made for?*
  To know God
- *What aim should we set for ourselves in life?*
  To know God
- *What is the eternal life that Jesus gives?*
  Knowledge of God
- *What is the best thing in life?*
  Knowledge of God
- *What in man gives God most pleasure?*
  Knowledge of Himself[3]

1. What's Packer's point?

2. Where are you on this grand scale of knowing God? Think about it, then give your honest, personal answer to each of these questions:
- What was I made for?
- What is my aim/goal in life?

- What does Christ's gift of eternal life mean to me?
- What is the best thing in life?
- What am I doing right now in my life that brings God the most pleasure?

HONING OUR OBSERVATION SKILLS

As I write these lessons, I am aboard a cruise ship homebound from Alaska. This week I have seen God's handiwork in the endless ocean, the majestic glaciers, a moose swimming across Glacier Bay. My mind has been filled with a worshipful chorus of *Elohim, Elohim, Elohim.*

Initially I felt camaraderie as I listened to the national park ranger's lecture about the majestic, timeless glacial formations, even referring to the glaciers by name. Suddenly, however, my reverie was shot out of the water as I realized her worldview included the creation minus the Creator. Then came her remark, "Have you hugged your pond scum today?" *Hugged my pond scum?* I wanted to leap out of my wheelchair and crawl onto the stage in the ship's crowded auditorium and rephrase the question, "Have you hugged *Elohim* today?"

I pray your awareness of who God is will sharpen with this study as your senses awaken to the multiple facets of God's presence in the world around you. To that end, in each chapter I provide a section for personal reflection on each of God's names. I also encourage you to keep a log of the times you are especially aware of Him in the "Hunt" provided at the end of each lesson, like the one shown here.

God Hunt: Treat yourself to a God Hunt.
Look for signs of His presence in Scripture, in
nature, in hymns, in others, in the mirror. . . .
Record how you have seen and enjoyed Him
during the week.

I saw _____

_____

_____

_____

*Date*_____

Finally, because music augments our worship of the many
aspects of God's Person, I end each lesson with a short list of
songs that highlight each particular name of God. I invite you
to add songs you love to the inexhaustible list and then sing to
the Lord accompanied by your instrument of choice or in con-
cert with a favorite vocal artist via CD or a music website such
as YouTube on the Internet.

A FEW MORE THINGS

This Bible Study is designed so that you may record your
thoughts and answers in this book, in a journal or a special file
on your computer. Whichever method you choose, be sure to
allow *growing room* so that you can chronicle how God shows
up in His mighty names year after year in your life.

Since the Hebrew names of God are not clearly represent-
ed in English Bibles, you might be wondering how you are sup-

posed to locate them without learning Hebrew and then reading a Hebrew Bible. One excellent resource is Ann Spangler's *The Names of God Bible* (NOG), which uses the Hebrew names as they occur. Oh, the joy of seeing the names of God in their scriptural context! I highly recommend purchasing this book to simplify and augment your study: *The Names of God Bible*, General Editor: Ann Spangler (Baker Publishing Group, 2011).

In addition, there are many good Internet resources. Two that I recommend are Bible Gateway (www.biblegateway. com), an online searchable Bible in dozens of versions, and Bible Hub (www.biblehub.com), an online parallel Bible with search and study tools.

Now jump in and get started! As you do, know that I am praying that the God whose grandeur requires oh-so-many names will become the Love of your life. And I pray that your study of His names results in a life-transforming, ever-empowering relationship between you and His Majesty.

Notes:

_____

_____

_____

_____

_____

_____

_____

_____

_____

_____

_____

_____

_____

_____

_____

_____

_____

_____

_____

_____

_____

_____

_____

*"In the beginning God created
the heavens and the earth."*

Genesis 1:1 NASB

2
Elohim

MIGHTY CREATOR

The Creator God Who Makes No Mistakes

BASIC FACTS

- The Hebrew word *El* means "mighty" or "strong."
- *El* + *him* indicates plurality, three or more, which some scholars believe to be a reference to the Trinity – Father, Son and Holy Spirit.
- *Elohim* does not denote many gods, but the mightiness of one true God. *"The Lord is our God (Elohim), the Lord is one!"* (Deuteronomy 6:4 NASB)
- *Elohim*, the source and maker of everything, appears 32 times in the 31 verses of Genesis, chapter 1, and an estimated 2,500 times in the Old Testament.[4]
- In most English versions of the Old Testament, the word *God* is the rendering for the Hebrew name *Elohim*.

ELOHIM IN THE BIBLE

1. *Elohim's* creation account is found in the first chapters of the Bible, Genesis chapters 1 and 2. The word *genesis* means "origins." Verse 1 of Genesis 1 states, *"In the beginning."* Identifying God as the Creator of all things, the chapter describes

the beginning of everything except God. He is eternal with no beginning and no end.

- How many times do you see "God" (*Elohim*) in Genesis 1 in your own Bible?

- God merely spoke and His words alone brought creation out of nothing. His light swallowed up darkness, and He lovingly created all things, including the human beings He made in His own image. Read Genesis chapter 1 and make a list of what God spoke into being.

Elohim, as the Creator, is foundational in the New Testament as well as the Old. It is interesting that the Gospel of John begins in the same way as Genesis with the phrase *in the beginning*. The apostle John's emphasis is on Jesus as the Creator.

- Read John 1:1-3, then John 1:14. Who is the Word? Is the Word God? What do these verses say about the Word and creation?

- The apostle Paul's letter to the Colossians further testifies to Jesus as Creator. Read and write out Colossians 1:16, then summarize it in your own words.

2. Remember Job, the righteous man who lost everything? He lost his children, his health and his wealth. Even when his wife told him to curse God and die, he stood up for God. Eventually his faith was worn down, however, by the accusations and "reasoning" of his three friends. (Friends? With friends like that who needs enemies?) But *Elohim* came to the rescue when He came a-calling in a whirlwind, giving Job a guided tour of His handiwork. *"Where were you when I laid the foundation of the earth?"* (Job 38:4 NASB) *"And where were you while the morning stars sang together and all the angels shouted for joy?"* (Job 38:7 NIV)

.

- Read Job chapters 38 and 39. Of all the created wonders *Elohim* describes, which ones grabbed your attention?

- Read about Job's worship-filled response in Job 42:1-6 after Creator God blasts Job's small view of God Almighty. Take special note of and comment on verse 5.

- Astronomers estimate that there are a billion trillion stars in the universe. The prophet Isaiah describes the tenderness *Elohim* feels toward His creation in 40:21-26. Enjoy this passage and record your thoughts about the intimacy God possesses toward what He's created, even the stars in the universe.

3. Getting more personal, Genesis 1:26-27 is a mind-boggling statement. What phrase is repeated three times about *Elohim* and His prize creation?

Imago Dei refers to God's design of you and me *in His likeness.* Unlike other things He created, we have the gift of spoken and written language and we bear the characteristics of spirituality, intelligence and creativity.

And yet, since the Fall, we are distorted image-bearers. Henrietta Mears said it well: "His image remains in us, though marred, but not an atom of His life. The divine nature of God becomes ours only when the divine Saviour becomes ours. With Christ in us God's divine nature is within us."[5]

- Where are you in terms of living up to God's intent that you bear His likeness? Are you doing okay, or do you need *Elohim's* help?

4. While you read Psalm 139 aloud, personalize it by putting your name in it.

- Verses 13-16 have been key to my recognizing my worth, birth defect and all. What do these verses say to you personally about *Elohim's* creation called YOU?

In the King James Version, verse 14 states, *"I am fearfully and wonderfully made."* (KJV)

- Where are you in terms of processing this? How does this truth impact your self-acceptance (being comfortable in your own skin)? How does this truth impact your self-worth (believing you have great worth)?

- For what aspects of the way *Elohim fearfully and wonderfully made* you are you thankful? With what aspects do you struggle?

5. Our Creator cares deeply about His creation. You just read in Isaiah that He calls each star by name. If He cares that much for the stars, imagine how great His love is for us! He knows when we need a tender lullaby to remind us of our great worth and His unending delight in us.

Worth? Delight? When I was over my head in motherhood, feeling totally inadequate and condemned, God's Spirit serenaded me through Zephaniah 3:17-18 (The Living Bible translation): *"The Lord God has arrived to live among you. He is a mighty savior. He will give you victory. He will rejoice over you in great gladness. He will love you and not accuse you. Is that a joyous choir I hear? No, it is the Lord Himself rejoicing over you in happy song."* (TLB)

- What do these verses tell you about God and His acts of love toward you His Beloved?

- Zephaniah was the prophet who heard God singing over him. When, if ever, have you heard God sing to you? Have you perhaps heard that serenade through a favorite hymn or praise song? Explain.

6. Sadly, God's prize creation – humanity – had rebelled and was expelled from the Garden of Eden by the end of Genesis chapter 3. But God's judgment on man's disobedience was met immediately with God's promise to restore the broken relationship. His rescue plan finds fulfillment in His only begotten Son, Jesus Christ.

Jesus came to earth to restore fellowship between Creator God and you and me. Fellowship is restored when we receive Him as our Savior, allowing Him to save us from our self-destructive course. The sky's the limit when we crown Him Lord and bow to Him as the Sovereign One, the Boss in our universe. Faith in Him results in our re-creation. We become a new creation in Him.

- Read and write out II Corinthians 5:17.

- Where are you in terms of II Corinthians 5:17? Are you in Christ or out of Christ?

- Can you identify a point in time when you became a new creation? It's wonderful when children turn to the Lord, but early decisions need to be actualized in adulthood. Some people can tell you the day, hour and minute of the beginning of their new life in Christ. Others look back on a time in their lives without remembering the exact day or hour. What is your re-creation story as an adult?

7. Read Ephesians 2:1-10, which describes our blessed condition when we say "yes" to becoming new creatures in Christ.

- Write out what your Bible says in verse 10.

- The New Living Translation of the Bible describes *new creatures in Christ* as God's masterpieces. You may be asking, "Me? A masterpiece?" How comfortable are you thinking of yourself as God's masterpiece?

- Other versions refer to us as God's workmanship. What does being God's workmanship mean to you?

8. The Greek word for masterpiece is *poema*, meaning we are God's poem. Mrs. Billy Graham's poem captures the wonder and mystery of this.

Odd this twisted form...

By Ruth Bell Graham

Odd
this twisted form
should be
the work of
God.
God
Who makes,
without mistakes,
the happy norm,
the status quo,
the usual,
made me,
you know.
The Royal Palm
He made;
and, too,
the stunted pine.
With joy
I see the lovely shapes.
With pride
I live in mine.

No accident I am:
a Master Craftsman's plan.[6]

- Comment on the paradox addressed in this poem.

- Are you surprised to learn that you are not an accident? How does the truth that the Master Craftsman planned you change your view of yourself?

9. *Elohim,* our Creator, has planted unique talents and abilities in each one of us, which reach their fullest potential when we yield our life to Him. But what about disabilities? We all have them. Some are visible but most are invisible. Broken bodies? Broken minds? Broken hearts? What about birth defects? Could it be God makes mistakes? Who's to blame?

- Read John 9:1-3 and write down Jesus' answer (verse 3).

- If you have some kind of disability you were born with, what do Jesus' words mean to you?

- If you are the parent of a child who was born with a disability, what do Jesus' words mean to you?

This question of cause can hunt us down in the dark. I love The Message Bible's translation of verse 3:

Jesus said, "You're asking the wrong question. You're looking for someone to blame. There is no such cause-effect here. Look instead for what God can do." (John 9:3 MSG)

- What in your life or the life of a loved one needs to be put to rest by Jesus' words, *"Look instead for what God can do"*?

10. If God is the Idea Person behind the universe, nature, invention, science – and He is – then He's the One to call on when we find ourselves lacking creative ideas or grappling for a solution to a problem. Each time we invite our creative Creator to be ruler in our lives, we become the recipients of His limitless power. When stuck, I've learned to say, *"Elohim,* the God of 1,000 ideas, I need You now."

- Is this the prayer of your heart today? If so, identify the area(s) of your life where you welcome *Elohim's* unlimited creativity.

- In what area(s) do you owe Him a thank you for His creativity in you and through you?

Elohim & You

1. Who is *Elohim* in your own words?

2. How has acknowledging *Elohim* as your personal Creator impacted your life?

3. Take some time to write a prayer, poem or Thank You letter to *Elohim*.

4. **God Hunt:** Treat yourself to an *Elohim* Hunt. Look for signs of His presence in Scripture, in nature, in hymns, in others, in the mirror. Invite Him to open your eyes to see His amazing creation in you and others. Record how you have seen His creativity as you face your daily challenges during the week.

I saw *Elohim* _____

_____

_____

Date _____

I saw *Elohim* _____

_____

_____

Date _____

I saw *Elohim* _____

_____

_____

Date _____

5. **A Songfest to *Elohim*:** Music can move words of truth from our heads to our hearts. Below are a few songs that high-light *Elohim*. Add your favorites, and then grab your instrument of choice or perhaps sing along with a CD or a YouTube video on the Internet. Make a joyful noise to *Elohim*!

How Great Thou Art
Indescribable
Fairest Lord Jesus
For the Beauty of the Earth
Morning Has Broken
This is My Father's World
The Wonder of It All

Add any of your favorites:

_____

_____

Notes:

"I call out to High God,
the God who holds me together."

Psalm 57:2 MSG

3

El Elyon

THE MOST HIGH GOD

*The God Who Gives Height and
Dignity to Our Low Places*

BASIC FACTS

- The Hebrew word *El* is singular, referring to God's might and strength.
- *El Elyon* is a superlative denoting the strongest of the strong.
- *El Elyon* is the Sovereign of the Universe; He is above all else, and all else is below Him.
- The Most High God is the Boss of the Universe; nothing happens without His permission.
- Our English Bible translations render *El Elyon* as *God Most High,* the *Lord Most High,* the *Most High God* or simply *Most High.*

EL ELYON IN THE BIBLE

1. *El Elyon* is first mentioned in Genesis 14:18-23 when Abram meets the mysterious Melchizedek, identified as the Priest of God Most High.

- Read the passage and identify how many times reference is made to the Most High God.

- How does Abram respond?

2. Balaam was a pagan prophet, actually a fool, who heard the voice of *El Elyon* through an unprecedented experience.

- Read Numbers 22:21-35. What did Balaam experience that opened his eyes and brought his acts of disobedience to a screaming halt?

- In Numbers 24:16 Balaam refers to _____.

3. Isaiah 14:12-16 is believed to be a passage describing Satan's (Lucifer's) rebellion against the Sovereign of the Universe. *El Elyon* is the very name that Satan uses in his defiance.

- List Satan's five declarations against God's authority.
    1.
    2.
    3.
    4.
    5.

Satan's rift with God comes down to a blatant refusal to acknowledge God as *El Elyon*. The universal power struggle with God both in heaven and on earth boils down to: *Who's the Boss?* We humans can be more subtle but just as arrogant, as we play God and try to run our own lives.

- Take time to assess your own personal rebellion – a heart attitude that declares, "God, You aren't the boss of me." Are there specific areas where you refuse to let Him reign? Write down what comes to mind.

4. It's interesting to note how Lucifer had no trouble recognizing *El Elyon* for who He is, nor did his demons.

- Read Luke 8:26-39. How does the demon, Legion, identify Jesus in verse 28?

To recognize something and to own up to that something are as different as lightning and a lightning bug. Satan and his demons recognize *El Elyon* but refuse to bow to Him. In rebellion they consider themselves the High and Mighty. They lack the heart attitude described in Isaiah 57:15 and Psalm 51:17.

- Read the two verses in Isaiah and Psalms, then describe the kind of heart that God desires in you.

5. James 4:6 says that *"God is opposed to the proud, but gives grace to the humble."* (NASB) The first six chapters of Daniel validate this kingdom principal as the faith of four lowly slaves introduces a mighty earthly king to the mightier King of Heaven. King Nebuchadnezzar's journey to faith is a classic study in God's humbling of the proudest of the proud.

- Read Daniel chapter 3. Who did King Nebuchadnezzar see show up to save the day for Shadrach, Meshach and Abednego (Daniel 3:26 and 4:2)?

- The king's journey to faith continues in Daniel 4:1-37 as a Hebrew slave boy named Daniel does what no one else can do: interpret the king's complicated dream. Describe King Nebuchadnezzar's heart transformation from high and mighty worship of self in verse 30 to humble worship of *El Elyon* in verses 34-37.

- Getting up close and personal, what are you high and mighty about? Whom are you high and mighty toward?

- Are you willing to invite *El Elyon* to perform a Nebuchadnezzar transformation in your own life? If so, record your request here.

6. *EI Elyon,* the Sovereign of heaven and earth, is the Owner of everything in His Kingdom. It all belongs to Him. How many of us quote Psalm 50:10, declaring that our God owns the cattle on 1,000 hills, but fail to recognize He owns the clothes in our closet, the money in our wallet, the car in our garage, our home, our children. *Yikes, He owns me!*

Interesting how He owns each one of us but gives us free will to choose Him or reject Him. How patiently He waits for us, His created ones, to come down from our high and mighty throne and finally hand over the deed of ownership to our lives. How glorious the day when we dethrone our arrogance and humbly choose to acknowledge, "I'm all Yours, Lord."

- Right now – today – who holds the deed to your life? What does that mean to you?

- If you have done so, share the details of when you returned the deed of your life to its Rightful Owner. What did it take to get you to the place where you were willing to bow to Him as the Most High God?

- Maybe you're still holding the deed but are ready to do business with *El Elyon* right now. Remember, a humble heart attitude is what counts. Are you ready to pray this simple prayer? "God, I acknowledge You as the Boss of the Universe and the Boss of me."

7. Think of it – the Most High God stood His tallest on an old rugged cross. You and I stand our tallest seated on his shoulders.

- Do you know how it feels to be nestled atop *El Elyon's* shoulders? What does He whisper in your ear while you are up there?

Because we are *El Elyon's* beloveds, His height and dignity become our height and dignity, and we find ourselves standing tall no matter what our stature.

- Shorty Zacchaeus in the New Testament was singled out of the crowd by Jesus, the Most High God. Read Luke 19:1-10 and comment on how Zacchaeus' height was altered by his encounter with Jesus.

- How has your height and dignity been impacted since becoming a Christ follower? Give specifics.

8. The Bible teaches that "being too short" (falling short) is a universal problem.

- Read Romans 3:23 and write down what it says. What does the verse mean to you personally?

No matter what our height, we all fall short of *El Elyon*. But He offers a cure for Shorties: The Most High God became short so we could become tall. Jesus Himself became a Shorty, willingly humbling Himself, knowing that God's way up is down.

- Read Philippians 2:5-8 and describe the stages of the Son of God's downward descent.

- Now read verses 9-11 and highlight the Heavenly Father's rewards for His Son's voluntary humiliation.

- How has this kingdom principle – that God's way up is down – been evident in your own experience (or the experience of another)?

9. In his account of Jesus' birth, Luke tells of the angel Gabriel visiting a lowly peasant girl named Mary and foretelling her role as mother of Jesus.

- Read Luke 1:26-38. According to verse 32, what would the baby be called?

- In chapter 2:1-20 Luke describes *El Elyon's* humble arrival on earth, heralded by heaven's angelic alleluias the night He was born. Write out verse 14, the heavenly host's birth announcement of the King, and describe how it impacts you.

- Truly *El Elyon's* way up is down. Think of it:
  ◦ The angel's alleluias were sung to lowly shepherds (the outcasts in those days).
  ◦ The Sovereign of the Universe was born in a manger.
  ◦ God chose a peasant couple for His Son's earthly parents.
  ◦ A stinky stable was God's pick to receive the Holy One.
  What can you add to this list?

From a stinky stable to human hearts. Interesting how *El Elyon* longs for our rebellious hearts to become His earthly home. He wants to come in and eat with you – He says so in Revelation 3:20. That's the verse God used to help me (and many others) understand that He wanted a relationship with me. On the basis of that verse, I invited Jesus to be the Boss of my life.

- Read Revelation 3:20 and write what is says.

- Personalize this verse by putting your own name in it. How do Jesus' words relate to your life?

10. Once He has made His home in our hearts, *El Elyon* woos His beloved to a high calling.

- Look up Philippians 3:14, and write it here.

- Can you think of other verses that describe and define this privileged calling of God's set-apart children?

- Prayerfully consider and record your thoughts and feelings about your high calling in Christ. One excellent book to guide you as you pursue this calling is Oswald Chamber's ageless devotional, *My Utmost for His Highest*,[7] for which Philippians 3:14 is the foundational verse.

El Elyon & You

1. Who is *El Elyon* in your own words?

2. How has acknowledging *El Elyon* as the Boss of you impacted your life?

3. Take some time to write a prayer, poem or Thank You letter to *El Elyon*.

4. **God Hunt:** Treat yourself to an *EI Elyon* Hunt this week. Look for signs of His presence in Scripture, in nature, in hymns, in others, in the mirror. Invite Him to open your eyes to see His ownership of you and the world around you. Welcome his gifts of height and dignity, especially on down days. Record how you have seen Him display His might and strength this week.

I saw *El Elyon* _____

_____

_____

Date _____

I saw *El Elyon* _____

_____

_____

Date _____

I saw *El Elyon* _____

_____

_____

Date _____

5. **A Songfest to *El Elyon*:** Music can move words of truth from our heads to our hearts. Here are a few songs that highlight *El Elyon*. Add your favorites and then grab your instrument of choice or perhaps sing along with a CD or a YouTube video on the Internet. Make a joyful noise to *El Elyon*!

> *Humble Thyself in the Sight of the Lord*
> *Higher Ground*
> *You Raise Me Up*
> *Lord I Lift Your Name on High*
> *I'd Rather Have Jesus*
> *How Great is Our God*

Add any of your favorites:

_____

_____

Notes:

"Our help is in the name of the LORD,
the maker of heaven and earth."

Psalm 124:8 NASB

4

Jehovah

I AM WHO I AM

My Child: Whatever You Need, I AM

Basic Facts

- Holy God introduced Himself to Moses as *Jehovah* – the great I AM WHO I AM.
- The name *Jehovah* is the most frequently used Hebrew name in the Old Testament, occurring thousands of times.
- The name *Jehovah* refers to God's essence, His holiness.
- Religiously observant Jews considered the name *Jehovah* too holy to speak or write.
- *Jehovah* is usually rendered as Lord with capital letters in our English Bibles.

Jehovah in the Bible

1. Read Exodus 3:1-15 about Moses' *on-fire* encounter with God.

    - What is the memorial name with which God identified Himself in Exodus 3:14?

- Put yourself in Moses' sandals and describe your response to a burning bush that is not consumed, a bush that gives you unthinkable marching orders, a bush embodying the Holy One Himself.

2. Moses, who would have preferred that someone else fill his sandals, needed courage from above for the humanly impossible assignment given to him. But *Jehovah's* offer to Moses was, "Whatever you need, I AM," and He not only equipped him for the call, He companioned with him (Exodus 3:12) every step of the way.

- Looking back in your own life, share a time when you faced an impossible task that forced you to take God up on His offer, "Whatever you need, I AM." Did He come through for you? Did He walk with you every step of the way? Explain.

3. Read more of Moses' adventure in Exodus 4.

- Identify the verses conveying:
  - *Jehovah's* patience _____
  - Moses' unbelief _____
  - *Jehovah's* willingness to grow Moses' faith_____
    _____

50

- Now apply this to your own life. What task looms over you today? What does *Jehovah* say to you about that task?

4. Have you ever burst into praise-filled song upon successfully completing a humanly impossible task? Moses certainly did, after he and three-million-plus Israelites walked through the Red Sea on dry land and the Egyptian army chasing them was swallowed up by that same sea.

- Read Moses' "*Jehovah* is a Warrior" tribute in Exodus 15:1-18 and write down what stands out to you.

- In verse 11 Moses uses three phrases to describe his great *Jehovah*. What are they?
    1.
    2.
    3.

5. *Jehovah* and Moses have an amazing encounter in Exodus 33, after which the LORD describes His personal attributes to Moses. Read Exodus 34:5-7. What words does *Jehovah* use to describe Himself in these verses?

- Put a heart beside the above attributes for which you are most thankful.

- After *Jehovah* revealed His glory, what was Moses' response (Exodus 34:8-9)? Think of an instance when you could identify with that response.

6. David – the shepherd boy who became king – was a writer, thus his intimate relationship with *Jehovah* is preserved.

- Read and write down what David says about his *Jehovah* in I Chronicles 29:11-13. (Great verses to memorize!)

- In Psalm 103, David lists the benefits that are ours when we put *Jehovah* on the throne of our lives. Read Psalm 103:3-5 and write down the benefits you find.

7. "Whatever you need, I AM" is *Jehovah's* daily offer to each one of us.

- Read Isaiah 40:28-31. Describe the strength *Jehovah* wants to give you.

- In what area of your life are you depending on this supernatural strength right now?

- The LORD's words to Isaiah in chapter 43:1-3 are His

words to us. Personalize verse 2.

- Share a time when you have claimed this promise, or describe a situation where you can claim it right now.

8. The Great I AM of the Old Testament visits earth in the incarnation of God's Son, Jesus Christ. The book of John contains the seven I AMs of Jesus.

- What attribute of Jesus' deity does each of the following verses convey?
  - John 6:35
  - John 8:12
  - John 10:9
  - John 10:11
  - John 11:25
  - John 14:6
  - John 15:1

- Describe how Jesus has shown up in your life in any of these ways.

9. Jesus, *Jehovah* Incarnate, wants to meet all of our needs. Glorious is the day we realize that He is the only One who can! Contrary to popular belief, God does not help those who help

themselves. Rather, He waits until we realize we need His help. But first we have to admit we have a need.

- Read John 4:7-26, which contains Jesus' encounter with one of society's outcasts. Assess the Samaritan woman's realization of her need. Who does Jesus say that He is to her? What is her response?

- Is it easy for you to acknowledge your needs? Why or why not?

Hourly *Jehovah* invites us in our inadequacy to rely on His infinite resources. And when we accept His provisions, our holes (our broken or missing pieces) become filled with His wholeness and His holiness. All the resources of the Great I AM, the God of the Universe, become ours.

- In what area of your life do you need His limitless resources this week?

- Read and personalize Ephesians 3:20. Are His resources enough? How much can He do for you?

10. Holy God described Himself with the phrase "I AM WHO I AM," not "I AM WHAT I DO." And yet we humans are con-

sumed each day by what we need to do, what's gotten done and what's yet to be done. We believe the lie that we are what we do instead of the truth that we are who we are – beloved children of *Jehovah*.

- How about we start a revolutionary mindset? Write down how your days would be altered if you bookended each one with the words "I am His and He is mine."

Jehovah & You

1. Who is *Jehovah* in your own words?

2. How has acknowledging *Jehovah* as the Giver of whatever you need impacted your life?

3. Take some time to write a prayer, poem or Thank You letter to *Jehovah*.

4. **God Hunt:** Treat yourself to a *Jehovah* Hunt. Look for signs of His presence in Scripture, in nature, in hymns, in others, in the mirror. Invite Him to open your eyes to see His essence – the quintessence of who He is – within you and around you. Keep track of (and rejoice) every time your spirit says "YES" to His offer – "Whatever you need, I AM."

I saw *Jehovah* _____

_____

_____

Date _____

I saw *Jehovah* _____

_____

_____

Date _____

I saw *Jehovah* _____

_____

_____

Date _____

5. **A Songfest to *Jehovah*:** Music can move words of truth from our heads to our hearts. Below are a few songs that highlight *Jehovah*. Add your favorites, and then grab your instrument of choice or perhaps sing along with a CD or a YouTube video on the Internet. Make a joyful noise to *Jehovah*!

Holy, Holy, Holy
The Great I Am
God of Wonders
Standing on Holy Ground
Majesty
You Are Holy

Add any of your favorites:

_____

_____

Notes:

_____

_____

_____

_____

_____

_____

_____

_____

_____

_____

_____

_____

_____

_____

_____

_____

_____

_____

_____

_____

_____

_____

_____

_____

_____

_____

*"Because the LORD is my Shepherd,
I have everything I need!"*

Psalm 23:1 TLB

5

Jehovah Raah

THE LORD MY SHEPHERD

*The Shepherd God Who Cares
for Our Every Need*

BASIC FACTS

- *Jehovah Raah* means "the LORD my shepherd."
- The LORD My Shepherd is found in David's Psalm 23.
- Though the name appears only a few times throughout Scripture, our Shepherd's loving care permeates every page.
- The Bible likens God's people to sheep. For those who know the nature of sheep, the implication is obvious: We humans need a Shepherd.
- Jesus identifies Himself as the Good Shepherd.

JEHOVAH RAAH IN THE BIBLE

1. David, the earthly shepherd-king, memorializes the heavenly Shepherd-King in Psalm 23. The name *Jehovah Raah* appears in the first verse.

- God's bountiful provision toward each one of us might explain this psalm's popularity. As you read the psalm, take note of the action verbs, then list the many responsibilities *Jehovah Raah* places on Himself versus our responsibilities as believers. The first one is given as an example.

God's Responsibilities   *My Responsibilities*

He makes me to lie down   I am to trust Him

_____   _____

_____   _____

- For which provisions do you most want to thank the Shepherd?

2. The Bible is replete with references to sheep, shepherds and The Shepherd. As you read the following verses from the Old Testament, think about what they mean in terms of the sheep theme throughout the Bible. Put hearts by your favorites.

- God refers to us as what in Psalm 100:3c?

- Comment on Isaiah 40:11, which describes God's heart attitude toward each one of us.

- Isaiah 53:6a describes mankind's universal bent toward independence from *Jehovah Raah*. Cross out the words "us" and "we" in the verse, replace them with your name and read the verse out loud. Does this description fit you?

- The second half of the verse (Isaiah 53:6b) describes God's solution to every person's rebellion. What does this part of the verse mean? To whom does the pronoun "him" refer?

3. The sheep and shepherd theme carries over from the Old to the New Testament.

- Read John 10:10-16. What does Jesus define as His purpose in coming to earth in John 10:10b? How does He identify Himself in verses 11 and 14?

- We see Jesus' commitment to us in Matthew 9:36. Describe the emotion contained in this Shepherd's heart.

- Describe how you would feel if you had no Shepherd.

4. It's been said that God doesn't call us sheep because we are warm and cuddly. Write down what you know about sheep.

5. My knowledge of sheep has come from three sources: Phillip Keller's book, *A Shepherd Looks at Psalm 23*,[8] Susan Schoenian's article, Sheep 201: A Beginner's Guide to Raising Sheep[9] and from my niece Tiffany's stories about the sheep on her farm. My conclusions about the mentality and behavior of the sheep are the following:

- ◦ Sheep are helpless creatures unable to fend for themselves. They are high maintenance, requiring endless attention and meticulous care, always needing to be led and protected.
- ◦ When frightened, sheep panic. If left to their own devices, they'll get themselves into more trouble.
- ◦ Sheep lack the ability to reason themselves out of harm's way, so when faced with one danger they may run straight into another danger.
- ◦ Highly aware of their surroundings, sheep grow uneasy and nervous with change.

• Which of these characteristics resonate with you?

6. When you learn the true nature of sheep, you soon realize their survival is 100% dependent on their shepherd.

• Think about what it means to be 100% dependent. Are you completely trusting the Shepherd God who cares for you? What percent would you give yourself: "In all honesty, I trust God _____ percent of the time."

7. *Jehovah Raah* knows that as sheep we are prone to wander. How innocently can we lose sight of the Shepherd! And sometimes we purposely take off with great bravado. *Who me? I don't need a Shepherd!* But eventually we become frightened, craving the shelter and security of the Shepherd God who cares for our every need.

- Write out Psalm 119:176, which I call my "Shepherd, I need You now" verse.

- Describe a time you wandered off from the Shepherd. How did you feel? What happened to make you return?

8. In The Message, Psalm 119:176 reads: *"And should I wander off like a lost sheep—seek me! I'll recognize the sound of your voice."* (MSG)

- Give at least one example of a time you recognized the Shepherd's voice, or perhaps a time when He guided you without a word.

9. It is interesting that Jesus, who is our Good Shepherd, is also the sacrificial Lamb of God.

- As early as Genesis 22 reference is made to a lamb sacrifice. Read verses 1-14 and comment on verse 8.

- Jesus' role as a sacrificial lamb was announced publicly by His cousin, John the Baptist. Record John's description of Jesus in John 1:29.

10. The apostle John sees a vision of the resurrected Lamb and the Good Shepherd in the book of Revelation – a foretelling of what believers will see, thanks to the Lamb's sacrifice.

- Read Revelation 5:6-14 and comment on the glory and honor that is now bestowed on the Lamb.

- Now read Revelation 7:17 and explain how Jesus brought the concepts of Shepherd and Lamb together.

Jehovah Raah & You

1. Who is *Jehovah Raah* in your own words?

2. How has acknowledging *Jehovah Raah* as your own heavenly Shepherd-King impacted your life?

3. Take some time to write a prayer, a poem or a Thank You letter to *Jehovah Raah*.

4. **God Hunt:** Treat yourself to a *Jehovah Raah* Hunt. Look for signs of His presence in Scripture, in nature, in hymns, in others, in the mirror. Invite Him to open your eyes to see how He tenderly cares for your every need. Keep your ears tuned for His supportive cheers of "Raah, Raah, Raah" and record how you have seen the Shepherd-King during the week.

I saw *Jehovah Raah* _____

_____

_____

Date _____

I saw *Jehovah Raah* _____

_____

_____

Date _____

I saw *Jehovah Raah* _____

_____

_____

Date _____

5. **A Songfest to *Jehovah Raah*:** Music can move words of truth from our heads to our hearts. Below are a few songs that highlight *Jehovah Raah*. Add your favorites, and then grab your instrument of choice or perhaps sing along with a CD or a YouTube video on the Internet. Make a joyful noise to *Jehovah Raah*! Baa. Baa. Baa.

His Sheep Am I
Savior Like a Shepherd Lead Us
Shepherd of My Soul
The Lord is My Shepherd
Worthy is the Lamb That Was Slain
Lamb of God

Add any of your favorites:

_____

_____

Notes:

_____

_____

_____

_____

_____

_____

_____

_____

_____

_____

_____

_____

_____

_____

_____

_____

_____

_____

_____

_____

_____

_____

_____

"Lo, I am with you always,
even until the end of the age."

Matthew 28:20b NASB

6

Jehovah Shammah

THE LORD IS THERE

*No Matter Where You Are,
I Am with You*

BASIC FACTS

- *Jehovah Shammah* means "the LORD is there."
- God's Hebrew name *Jehovah Shammah* appears only in the book of Ezekiel.
- Although the name appears only once in the Bible, God is present on every page.
- Immanuel, Jesus' God-given name, captures the wonder of "the LORD is there" – God became man and dwelt with us.

JEHOVAH SHAMMAH IN THE BIBLE

1. *Jehovah Shammah* identified Himself as The LORD is There at a very low point in Jewish history. The prophet Ezekiel, along with his fellow countrymen, were in captivity in Babylon. Jerusalem had been destroyed and the Temple ransacked. The glory of God that filled the Temple in Solomon's day was gone. And yet God's glory showed up in the ruins. God's promise, "I'll be there," birthed hope in their captivity.

- Read Ezekiel 48:35, the end of Ezekiel's vision as well as the end of God's description of the future New Jerusalem. What name did the Spirit of God reveal to Ezekiel in the name of the new city?

- Examine the ruins of your own life (we all have them) and share if you wish. Remember God's promise: "No matter where you are, I am with you." Prayerfully ask God to reveal His presence in your hurt over something in the past, your despair over something in the present or your fear about something in the future.

2. *Jehovah Shammah* doesn't abandon us in the ruins of our lives. In fact, that's where many of us discover Him. Patriarch Jacob, the grandson of Abraham and son of Isaac, was a supplanter, a deceiver and a liar. And yet God loved Jacob.

- Read of Jacob's encounter with an up-close and personal God in Genesis 28:10-21. What did God promise Jacob in verse 15?

- What was Jacob's response to this amazing encounter?

- Keep in mind – God met Jacob while he was running for his life after he tricked his brother Esau out of his birthright and their father's blessing. What does this tell you about God?

- It's been said that Jacob's faith was initially a hand-me-down faith from his father Isaac and his grandfather Abraham, but it became firsthand faith during his ladder-to-heaven experience. What's the difference?

- Think about your progression to faith. Did it begin with the faith of your parents? When did it become your own and what does that mean?

3. The book of Psalms overflows with hope and joy, thanks to our ever-present *Jehovah Shammah.*

- Think on the following words from the New American Standard version of Psalm 73:28: *"But as for me, the nearness of God is my good . . . ."* (NASB) Explain what these words mean to you.

- I've always loved The Living Bible paraphrase of this verse, which reads: *"But as for me, I get as close to him as I can! I have chosen him and I will tell everyone about the wonderful ways he rescues me."* (TLB) What does your translation say?

- Read Psalm 139, a passage that oozes with God's intimate love for each one of us. He did not robotically build humanity on an assembly line. Instead He carefully and lovingly crafted us *in utero*. His 100% attention is with us always and there's no way to depart from His presence. After you read the psalm, write down three ways that God's omnipresence ministers to you in your life.

4. In her survey of the Bible called *What the Bible Is All About,* Henrietta Mears says that the prophet Isaiah's secret to all of his power lay in his vision in the temple.[10]

- Read Isaiah 6 and describe what happened in verses 1-3.

5. Isaiah's encounter with God surely bolstered his faith so that he could hold fast to *Jehovah Shammah* during the hard times ahead.

- Look up the following passages, which may be familiar favorites. What assurance do you find in each passage?
  ◦ Isaiah 40:28-31
  ◦ Isaiah 41:10
  ◦ Isaiah 43:2-3

6. After 400 years pass between the Old and New Testaments, God's silence is broken by a baby's cry.

- Read Isaiah 7:14 and Matthew 1:23 to see how Isaiah's prophecy is fulfilled with the birth of Jesus. The baby's name, Immanuel, means _____.

- What does Jesus promise in Matthew 28:20b as He returns to Heaven?

7. In the Old Testament, God's glory filled the temple and the city of Jerusalem, but in the New Testament *Jehovah Shammah* moves into our individual neighborhoods.

- Look up John 1:14. Where does the Word that became flesh dwell?

- And it's even better than that. Read I Corinthians 3:16. Where does the God of the Universe choose to dwell? Comment on your honored function as a believer in Jesus Christ.

8. Like Isaiah, the apostle John had a vision, which is recorded in the book of Revelation.

- Read and enjoy Revelation chapters 21 and 22. In verse 21:2, John sees the _____, which God revealed to Ezekiel (48:35b) as _____.

- What does Revelation 21:3 tell us about God's presence?
  And what does verse 4 promise?

9. Psalmist David glories in *Jehovah Shammah* in Psalm 16.

- Note in particular his comment in verse 11b. According
  to David, where does he find joy?

- Getting up close and personal, share a time when you
  have felt joy in the Lord's presence.

10. The second chapter of Acts describes the day of Pentecost,
where God's Spirit came to indwell believers. The Spirit-filled
apostle Peter, who shortly before denied knowing Jesus Christ,
preaches his first sermon, which brings 3,000 people to faith.

In Acts 2:25-28 Peter quotes from Psalm 16:8-11. Years
ago I memorized these verses from The Message translation:

> *I saw God before me for all time.*
> *Nothing can shake me; he's right by my side.*
> *I'm glad from the inside out, ecstatic;*
> *I've pitched my tent in the land of hope.*
> *I know you'll never dump me in Hades;*
> *I'll never even smell the stench of death.*
> *You've got my feet on the life-path, with your*
> *face shining sun-joy all around.*

- Look up Acts 2:25-28 in your own Bible, then answer this question: What would make Peter, 3,000 people, you and me want to be in relationship with the God described in this passage?

Jehovah Shammah & You

1. Who is *Jehovah Shammah* in your own words?

2. How has acknowledging *Jehovah Shammah* as your LORD who is always there with you impacted your life?

3. Take some time to write a prayer, poem or Thank You letter to *Jehovah Shammah*.

4. **God Hunt:** Treat yourself to a *Jehovah Shammah* Hunt. Look for signs of His presence in Scripture, in nature, in hymns, in others, in the mirror. Invite Him to open your eyes to see Him in unexpected places. Record how you have seen Him with you during the week.

I saw *Jehovah Shammah* _____

_____

_____

Date _____

I saw *Jehovah Shammah* _____

_____

_____

Date _____

I saw *Jehovah Shammah* _____

_____

_____

Date _____

5. **A Songfest to *Jehovah Shammah*:** Music can move words of truth from our heads to our hearts. Below are a few songs that highlight *Jehovah Shammah*. Add your favorites, and then grab your instrument of choice or perhaps sing along with a CD or a YouTube video on the Internet. Make a joyful noise to *Jehovah Shammah*!

God Be with You
In This Very Room
God with Us
You Never Let Go
Alone Yet Not Alone

Add any of your favorites:

_____

_____

Notes:

_____

_____

_____

_____

_____

_____

_____

_____

_____

_____

_____

_____

_____

_____

_____

_____

_____

_____

_____

_____

_____

_____

*"For the eyes of the Lord search
back and forth across the whole earth,
looking for people whose hearts are perfect
toward him, so that he can show his
great power in helping them."*

II Chronicles 16:9 TLB

7

El Roi

THE GOD WHO SEES

*The God Who Companions
with Us in Our Pain*

BASIC FACTS

- *El Roi* means "the God who sees."
- *El Roi* visits Hagar, a cast-aside Egyptian slave, in the book of Genesis.
- Genesis 16:13 is the only place the name appears in Scripture but God's attribute of seeing and caring appears throughout.

EL ROI IN THE BIBLE

Does God care? Have you ever asked yourself that question? Have you ever wondered when you have been hurt or abandoned: *Does the God of the Universe give a hoot about me?*

1. Surely Hagar had those thoughts – alone in the wilderness, friendless, discarded like a soiled worthless rag, a runaway Egyptian slave. Her gods of Egypt were stone-faced and could only stare back at her. She was a most unlikely candidate for a visit from *El Roi,* the God who companions with us in our pain.

- Read Genesis 16 and meet Hagar. Describe what happened to her in the first 6 verses.

- Who visited her in the wilderness (verses 7-8)?

- What did He tell Hagar to do (verse 9)?

- What name was she told to give her unborn child (verse 11) and what does that name mean (verse 11b)?

- In verse 13 Hagar gives her visitor the name _____ _____.

2. After her son is weaned, *El Roi* visits Hagar again when He hears and responds to her son Ishmael's crying in the desert.

- Read Genesis 21:14-19. What does the God who sees do in verse 19?

- Can you identify with Hagar as an outcast? In what way?

- Possibly someone you love has been cast out like a dirty rag. Often, seeing the pain of one we love hurts more than our own pain. Put yourself in Hagar and Ishmael's sandals and write down how you imagine God would companion with the two of you in your pain.

3. The God who sees not only sees but actively responds to affliction. He responded to the affliction of an Egyptian slave and then later to the affliction of His people, enslaved in Egypt.

- Read Exodus 3:7-8. What did *El Roi* see?

- How did He respond to what He had seen?

- Share how *El Roi* has seen and responded to a long-lasting affliction of your own.

4. The psalmist David, who was an outcast for part of his life, describes the God who sees everything in his much-loved Psalm 139.

- Read verses 1-6, and make note of the verbs David uses to convey how *El Roi* oversees every detail of his life.

- What is David's response to this God who companioned with him so intimately (verse 6)? What is your response to this same God who companions with you?

5. *El Roi* took up residency on earth in the person of Jesus Christ. The New Testament Gospels give testimony to His tender heart toward the world's outcasts. Identify the outcasts in the following passages.

- Luke 17:12-19 _____
- Luke 18:35-43 _____
- Luke 19:1-10 _____
- Can you think of other outcasts from Scripture?

_____

_____

6. Ironically, Jesus Himself was cast out during His thirty-three years on earth. The innkeeper assigned Him to a stinky stable the night of His birth. The Jewish leaders rejected Him as their Messiah. He was deserted by His friends, crucified outside the Holy City and buried in a borrowed grave.

- Read and comment on Isaiah 53:7-9, a passage that foretells the death of Jesus.

- What is your reaction to the God who sees affliction becoming the afflicted one?

- Read and comment on II Corinthians 5:21. Why did Jesus become the afflicted one?

7. I don't expect to see Jesus this side of heaven, not with my physical eyes anyway. But I remember clearly how the blinders fell off my *spiritual eyes* when I made the decision to receive Christ into my life. Suddenly the Bible made sense and I just couldn't get enough of it. Christian Christmas carols came alive as God's Spirit gave me eyes to see the Christ of Christmas. I do believe God answered the apostle Paul's prayer found in Ephesians 1:18-19 in my life.

- Read and summarize Paul's prayer.

- Has God answered this prayer in your life? Be specific.

8. Sometimes our affliction is of our own making, due to our refusal to obey God's commands. Man's rebellion and disobedience are recorded as early as the third chapter of the Bible. And yet God seeks us out.

- Look up II Chronicles 16:9a. What does this tell you about the compassion in God's eyes and heart?

- What is He looking for?

- What does He want to do?

9. *El Roi* is a God who doesn't miss a thing. He sees and hears the good, the bad and the ugly in each one of our lives. And yet He loves us, and even seeks us out! And when we finally see Him, His message is one of love and forgiveness, not condemnation, because of what Jesus did on the cross for us. An Old Testament prophet said God will *"hurl all our iniquities into the depths of the sea."* (Micah 7:19b NIV) Corrie ten Boom has added, "Then God places a sign out there that says 'No Fishing Allowed!'" [11]

- Could it be you have something heavy on your heart that you need to hand over to the God who companions with you in your pain? Prayerfully consider what that might be, and record your thoughts here if you wish.

- Feel the relief as you watch Him hurl your bad and ugly into the depths of the sea. Take heed of the "No Fishing" sign. Now lean in close and listen. What is *El Roi* saying to you?

El Roi & You

—●•●—

1. Who is *El Roi* in your own words?

2. How has acknowledging *El Roi* as the God who sees your personal pain impacted your life?

3. Take some time to write a prayer, poem or Thank You letter to *El Roi*.

4. **God Hunt:** Treat yourself to an *El Roi* Hunt. Look for signs of His seeing and caring in Scripture, in nature, in hymns, in others, in the mirror. Invite Him to open your eyes to see when He companions with you in your pain. Record how you have seen Him watch over you during the week.

I saw *El Roi* _____

_____

_____

Date _____

I saw *El Roi* _____

_____

_____

Date _____

I saw *El Roi* _____

_____

_____

Date _____

5. **A Songfest to *El Roi*:** Music can move words of truth from our heads to our hearts. Here are a few songs that highlight *El Roi*. Add your favorites and then grab your instrument of choice or perhaps sing along with a CD or a YouTube video on the Internet. Make a joyful noise to *El Roi*!

In Heaven's Eyes
Open My Eyes That I May See
His Eye is on the Sparrow
You Are the God Who Sees
What a Friend We Have in Jesus
You Are for Me

Add any of your favorites:

_____

_____

Notes:

_____

_____

_____

_____

_____

_____

_____

_____

_____

_____

_____

_____

_____

_____

_____

_____

_____

_____

_____

_____

_____

_____

_____

_____

*"I'll let out lungsful of praise,
my rescued life a song."*

Psalm 71:23 MSG

8

Jehovah Nissi

THE LORD IS MY BANNER

The God Who Crowns Us a Winner

BASIC FACTS

- *Jehovah Nissi* means "the LORD is my banner."
- Moses built an altar naming it *Jehovah Nissi* in Exodus 17.
- Although the name appears only once in the Old Testament, the LORD's banner of victory appears repeatedly.

JEHOVAH NISSI IN THE BIBLE

1. Moses experienced *Jehovah Nissi's* victory when Amalek came and fought against Israel. Since God's agrarian people were not warriors, they definitely needed a miracle. Read the details of this battle in Exodus 17:8-16.

- Who led the fight on the battlefield (verses 9-10)?

- What did Moses do to aid in the battle (verse 9)?

- How did Moses' actions affect the battle (verse 11)?

- Who came to the rescue when Moses' arms became tired, and what did they do (verse 12)?

- What did Moses build after the Amalekites were defeated, and what did he name it (verse 15)?

2. In this account of the defeat of the Amalekites, it is clear that *Jehovah Nissi,* the God who crowns us a winner, is a firm believer in team work. In this situation, the team consisted of _____ on the battlefield and _____ on the mountain raising the banner with the help of _____ and _____.

- Share an example in your life when you were able to accomplish something only because of the help of others.

- Who's on your team now to help you win the daily battles? More specifically, who are your Aaron and Hur?

- Are you now on someone else's team? Share how you have had to rely on *Jehovah Nissi's* strength to serve as Aaron or Hur in someone else's battles.

3. "A banner in ancient times was not necessarily a flag such as we use nowadays. Often it was a bare pole with a bright shining ornament which glittered in the sun."[12]

- We see such a banner in Numbers 21:4-9. What resulted when the Israelites grumbled against the LORD?

- What were *Jehovah Nissi's* instructions to Moses in verses 8 and 9?

- For those who obeyed those instructions, how did God crown them as winners?

4. In the New Testament, Christ was placed on a pole – actually, a cross. In a conversation with Nicodemus, Jesus compares the bronze serpent in Numbers with His own destiny.

- Read John 3:14-15. Explain how faith brings life.

The banner – the power source – in Numbers 21 is a pole with a bronze serpent atop. When their eyes gazed upon the serpent, the Israelites were healed physically. The power source in the New Testament is a cross with Christ upon it. When our eyes of faith gaze at the cross of Christ, we are healed spiritually.

• What does this mean to you personally?

5. There is something more in the biblical account of Israel's battle against Amalek. Exodus 17:16b says, *"The LORD will be at war against the Amalekites from generation to generation."* (NASB) Believe it or not, this verse is of great significance in our daily walk with the LORD.

    • First of all, Amalek was a grandson of Esau. Read Genesis 25:19-34 to refresh your memory about Esau. What does Esau do in this passage? What does his action demonstrate? Is he more concerned with the "here and now" or the "there and later"?

    • Both Esau and his down-the-road grandson Amalek display humanity's bent to put self instead of God at the center of our lives. Our daily test is whether we will grab for instant gratification with the world's pleasures or enjoy delayed gratification with eternal treasures. How would you grade yourself on this test? Why?

6. Paul describes every believer's battle in Romans 7:18-19.

    • What is the universal problem according to this passage?

I know the battle well. That's probably what led me to dig deeper in the Exodus 17 passage. The comic strip character Pogo almost got it right when he said: "I have met the enemy and he is us." Not us, Pogo – the enemy is *me*! The Bible calls it the flesh. Although many of us casually refer to it as our ego, our pride or our strong will, *Jehovah Nissi* considers it a serious enemy.

- My personal battlefield has been my longing to be independent and self-sufficient instead of Legless Judy, the Short One always needing a boost. What is yours? In what specific area does your battle rage?

7. The truth is: we can't win the battle against our flesh in our own strength. The battle belongs to the LORD our Banner.

- Read Romans 7:24-25. Who changed Paul's discouragement to a victory cry?

When our eyes of faith gaze at Christ's victory on the cross, we are saved. But there is more: As believers we must die to our flesh. Galatians 2:20 explains the process – I die to my flesh; Christ lives in me.

- Read and write out the Galatians 2:20.

- Describe a specific time when you intentionally chose to

die to your flesh and thus experienced Christ's life in you.

- Take time to seriously consider this next question: What insidious habit or bitter-root attitude do you need to put to death? With the LORD as your Banner, nail that to the cross of Christ right now.

8. Jesus Himself further explains the process in Luke 9:23. These words burned into my soul as I faced the daily demands of self-sacrifice as I mothered three little children.

- Read Luke 9:23. What did Jesus say His followers must do?

- In what specific area is *Jehovah Nissi* calling you to live this out right now?

9. God wins our battles but crowns us the winners. Following His example, we win by losing (Luke 9:24). When our flesh steps out of the way, *Jehovah Nissi* steps in. He gave our marching orders to Moses in Deuteronomy.

- Read Deuteronomy 20:3-4 in your own Bible, then personalize the passage by filling in the blanks with your name and your enemies (your challenges or struggles) in the following author's paraphrase.

Yo! _____, listen up!
You are getting ready to battle against
_____, _____ and _____.
Don't be timid; don't shake in your boots.
No need to panic – I've got this!
I am going ahead of you and will be with you.
I am the Lord your banner!
I will fight for you against these enemies
and will crown you a winner.
Your job is to trust Me.

Love, Jehovah Nissi

Jehovah Nissi & You

———•⦁•———

1. Who is *Jehovah Nissi* in your own words?

2. How has acknowledging *Jehovah Nissi* as your personal banner and the One who crowns you a winner impacted your life?

3. Take some time to write a prayer, poem or Thank You letter to *Jehovah Nissi*.

4. **God Hunt:** Treat yourself to a *Jehovah Nissi* Hunt. Look for signs of His presence in Scripture, in nature, in hymns, in others, in the mirror. Accept His offer to win your battles and welcome heartily the team members He assigns to help you. Record how you have seen Him both infuse you with His strength and crown you a winner during the week.

I saw *Jehovah Nissi* _____

_____

_____

Date _____

I saw *Jehovah Nissi* _____

_____

_____

Date _____

I saw *Jehovah Nissi* _____

_____

_____

Date _____

5. **A Songfest to *Jehovah Nissi*:** Music can move words of truth from our heads to our hearts. Here are a few songs that highlight *Jehovah Nissi*. Add your favorites and then grab your instrument of choice or perhaps sing along with a CD or a YouTube video on the Internet. Make a joyful noise to *Jehovah Nissi*!

> *A Mighty Fortress is Our God*
> *His Banner over Me is Love*
> *No Man is an Island*
> *The Battle Belongs to the Lord*
> *Onward Christian Soldiers*

Add any of your favorites:

_____

_____

Notes:

"*For the* Lord *takes pleasure in His people;*
He will beautify the afflicted
ones with salvation."

Psalm 149:4 NASB

9

Jehovah Tsidkenu

THE LORD OUR RIGHTEOUSNESS

The God Who Can Right All Our Wrongs

BASIC FACTS

- *Jehovah Tsidkenu* means "the LORD our righteousness."
- The name first appears in the Old Testament in Jeremiah chapter 23.
- Although the name appears in only one place in Scripture, the reality of God's righteousness is a red thread woven throughout.
- In the New Testament, Christ on the cross is The LORD Our Righteousness.

JEHOVAH TSIDKENU IN THE BIBLE

1. I believe I hear the "Hallelujah Chorus" in the Genesis account of creation. Do you hear it? The crescendo is surely God's masterpiece – "*man and woman He created them.*" Too quickly, however, the glory fades and fellowship with Holy God is broken by Adam and Eve's disobedience. Read Genesis 3 to refresh your memory about how sin entered the world.

- In Genesis 3:14-24, God dispenses the consequences for Adam and Eve's sin. The worst of it is described in verse 23. Read that verse. Tell why that action was so terrible.

- The sin that broke mankind's relationship with God only got worse as time went on. Read and comment on Genesis 6:6. Would you say that God takes sin seriously?

2. Man's self-centeredness and rebellion are evident from Adam and Eve on. God's Word doesn't hide the truth, even though it's not a pretty picture. Examine the following passages.

- Read Isaiah 64:6-7a and explain God's assessment of the human condition.

- Describe humanity's heart disease in Jeremiah 17:9.

- According to Romans 3:23, how many miss the mark?

- What is your personal response to these verses?

3. Fortunately for us, the story doesn't end there. God knew we needed help. He knew we needed a Savior – Someone to

right all our wrongs. He promised He would send One; He did.

- Examine Jeremiah 23:5-6. What name is revealed to Jeremiah in verse 6?

- Six centuries later this prophecy was fulfilled by Jesus. According to Matthew 1:21, what does Jesus' name mean?

- Read Romans 5:8 and I Peter 2:24. How would *Jehovah Tsidkenu's* plan to right our wrongs play out?

4. Atonement is the theological term referring to the reconciliation between Creator and creation through the forgiveness of sin made possible by the death and resurrection of Jesus Christ. My down-to-earth, favorite definition of reconciliation is simply: God makes people to be His friends. But how?

- II Corinthians 5:21 provides the nuts and bolts of God's plan of salvation. I love the Living Bible's rendering: *"For God took the sinless Christ and poured into him our sins. Then, in exchange, he poured God's goodness into us!"* (TLB) Read the verse in your own Bible, and write what your translation says.

- What do those words mean to you?

5. It's been called The Great Exchange. My pastor friend Don Needham recently said, "It's the MOST one-sided exchange of all times. We got Jesus' best and He got our worst. We got His garment; He got our rags."

- Read Isaiah 64:6a again. What does it say about any righteous acts we might try to give Jesus in this exchange?

- What does Isaiah 61:10 say about the garment that Christ gives to those who believe?

6. The Son of God achieved the impossible and became the only bridge across the Grand Canyon of Sin that separates Holy God and sinful man.

- Jesus explained it to His disciples during their last supper together. What did He say in John 14:6?

- The apostle Peter, filled with the Holy Spirit, preached the same message in Acts 4:12. What did he say?

7. John 3:16, a verse familiar to many of us, summarizes *Je-*

hovah Tsidkenu's plan to save us from our self-destructive sin.

- Read the verse or recall it from memory and answer these questions.
  - How did God feel toward His broken creation?
  - What did He do about it?
  - What's our part in the plan?
  - What's the result when we do our part?

8. Throughout the book of Acts it is faith in the finished work of Jesus Christ – His death on the cross, His resurrection and His ascension into heaven – that is preached.

- Read Acts 16:22-34. What did Paul and Silas tell the terrified jailer after a great earthquake opened the prison doors and loosed the prisoners' chains? Write out Paul's specific words in Acts 16:31.

Believe on the Lord Jesus. . . . But, what does it mean to believe? I appreciate the way The Amplified Bible expands on the word *believe* in Acts 16:31: *"Give yourself up to Him; take yourself out of your own keeping and entrust yourself to His keeping."* (AMP)

To think I almost missed it, even having grown up as a PK (preacher's kid). I had faithful attendance in Sunday School, owned a dusty Bible and had even memorized John 3:16. I had a religion that lacked vitality. I didn't know about trading in my rags for His robe of righteousness. Then I finally hit the wall and reached the end of my rope in college. That's when my Aunt Ginny told me, "Believe on the Lord Jesus Christ and you will be saved," and I finally understood. That's when I graduated from knowledge about God to having faith in Him. That's when *Jehovah Tsidkenu* became MY *Jehovah Tsidkenu* and I became His.

- Have you given yourself up, allowing Christ's righteousness to become your own? Explain your answer.

9. *Jehovah Tsidkenu's* offer to replace our rags with Christ's robe is an offer to all humanity, but it is a gift that requires our personal acceptance. To exchange our unrighteousness for Christ's righteousness requires an act of the will.

- Read John 1:12. What two things are required to become a child of God robed in Christ?

Belief or unbelief. Acceptance or rejection. It's one or the other. Note how the two choices were played out while Jesus was dying on the cross, at the very time He was making salvation possible.

- Read Luke 23:39-43 and describe each of the criminals' responses to Jesus.

- What did Christ promise to the man who believed?

- And, going back to John 3:16, what does the God who can right all our wrongs promise to all future generations of believers?

10. Believe on the Lord Jesus, and you will be saved. . . . You may be holding back because you think your dastardly deeds are off the charts and unforgivable. If so, Max Lucado has the following words for you:

> Our Saviour kneels down and gazes upon the darkest acts of our lives. But rather than recoil in horror, he reaches out in kindness and says, "I can clean that if you want." And from the basin of his grace, he scoops a palm full of mercy and washes our sin.[13]

If you have never received *Jehovah Tsidkenu* as your righteousness, now would be a grand time to do so. You simply need to pray something like this from your heart: "Lord Jesus, I admit to You that I have sinned and I know I need a Savior. I believe You are the Son of God who died for my sins and rose again. I would like to exchange my rags for Your robe of righteousness. I am ready to give myself up to You and entrust myself to Your keeping."

- Did you pray that prayer just now? If so, welcome to the family of God. At your request God in the form of the Holy Spirit has taken up permanent residency in your life. Rest assured, you are His no matter what. Look up Hebrews 13:5b and record the Lord's commitment to you.

- If you have prayed a prayer like that before, share a little about the time and place, and about how your life changed after you made The Great Exchange.

Jehovah Tsidkenu & You

1. Who is *Jehovah Tsidkenu* in your own words?

2. How has acknowledging *Jehovah Tsidkenu* as your personal Righteous One impacted your life?

3. Take some time to write a prayer, poem or Thank You letter to *Jehovah Tsidkenu*.

4. **God Hunt:** Treat yourself to a *Jehovah Tsidkenu* Hunt. Look for signs of His righteousness and saving work in Scripture, in nature, in hymns, in others, in the mirror. Accept His promise to right your wrongs as you trust Him to be your Righteousness. Record how you have seen Him do just that during the week.

I saw *Jehovah Tsidkenu* _____

_____

_____

Date _____

I saw *Jehovah Tsidkenu* _____

_____

_____

Date _____

I saw *Jehovah Tsidkenu* _____

_____

_____

Date _____

5. **A Songfest to *Jehovah Tsidkenu*:** Music can move words of truth from our heads to our hearts. Here are a few songs that highlight *Jehovah Tsidkenu*. Add your favorites, and then grab your instrument of choice or perhaps sing along with a CD or a YouTube video on the Internet. Make a joyful noise to *Jehovah Tsidkenu*!

Amazing Grace
When I Survey the Wondrous Cross
Wonderful Grace of Jesus
There is Power in the Blood
Nothing but the Blood
And Can It Be?
Glory to His Name

Add any of your favorites:

_____

_____

Notes:

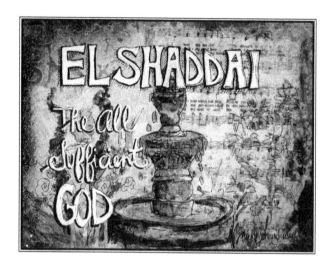

"If you return to the Almighty,
you will be restored. . . . "

Job 22:23 NASB

10

El Shaddai

THE ALL-SUFFICIENT GOD

The God Whose Supply Exceeds Life's Demands

BASIC FACTS

- *El Shaddai* appeared to Abram in Genesis 17:1.
- The name conveys a God who is both strong and tender.
- The name *El Shaddai* is most often rendered The All-Sufficient God, but also includes the All-Bountiful One who pours forth blessings.[14]
- The root word *shad* literally means "breast," signifying a God who nourishes, supplies, satisfies.[15]
- The name *El Shaddai* appears 30 times in the book of Job and a total of 48 times in the Old Testament.

EL SHADDAI IN THE BIBLE

1. The writer of Psalm 91 mentions two Hebrew names of God in verse 1; the first is *El Elyon* and the second is _____. Read the entire psalm and write down at least ten benefits that are ours as we "*spend the night in Shaddai's shadow*" (Psalm 91:1 MSG).

2. Abram is the father of the Judeo-Christian faith. Imagine his faith challenge as God's promise to make him a great nation is coupled with his wife Sarai's infertility. Though sorely tested, his faith remained strong.

- Read Genesis 15:4-6. Comment on Abram's response to the promise of God as well as God's response to Abram (verse 6).

- In Genesis 17, God appears again to Abram to reassure him about the yet-to-be-fulfilled promise. God identifies Himself as _____ (verse 1).

- Read Genesis 17:17 to determine the age of these senior-citizen parents: Abraham: _____;
his wife: _____. What an impossible situation! But now read the joyful news of Genesis 21:1-3. Did *El Shaddai* come through? Explain.

- Where has the All-Sufficient God of the Impossible come through in your life?

- In what impossibility are you still waiting for Him to show up?

3. The name *El Shaddai* is commonly linked to the strength of God Almighty. However, because *shad* means "breast," some Hebrew scholars stress His calming, nurturing, caring and protecting attributes. Like a mother nursing her helpless infant, God wants to provide for us.

- Obviously Sarai longed to nurse an infant at her breast. Do you think she was calmed by *El Shaddai* during her long wait for motherhood? Why or why not?

I personally met *El Shaddai* while nursing three consecutive infants in a five-year period. He showed up daily as I faced impossible feats without feet. Sweet was His presence and His promise: "I am *El Shaddai*, and I'll more than provide for your needs."

- What about you? Share a special time or event of your life where you met this nurturing, all-sufficient God.

4. The All-Sufficient God is all over the pages of the Old Testament book of Job. Job was inadequate to prevent or rectify the catastrophic events recorded in Job chapter 1. *El Shaddai* became his All-in-All as his wife and three friends beat him down.

- Read Job 22:23-26. How many times do you count the word *Almighty*?

- Read Job 22:25 and 23:10. Gold is mentioned in both verses. Comment on the dual reward when a believer suffers under *Shaddai's* shadow.

- Now read Job 42:5 and comment on Job's new level of relationship with the One who nourishes, supplies and satisfies us when we've lost all that is dear to us on earth.

- A deeper relationship with *El Shaddai* – that in itself would have been worth the suffering! But don't miss God's outpouring of blessings in Job 42:10-17. Describe how Job came out ahead.

5. In the book of Ruth, we meet *El Shaddai* with Naomi. Now a widow, she had once nursed two sons at her breasts, but they like her husband were dead. She and her two widowed daughters-in-law faced a bleak, seemingly hopeless future.

- Read Ruth 1:20. What three names are mentioned? What does each name mean?

When our pleasant life turns bitter, may we all know the presence *El Shaddai*. The short book of Ruth is well worth the read to see how the God whose supply exceeds life's demands turns Naomi's tragedy into a joyful celebration.

- Read the end of the story in Ruth 4:16-17. Naomi, who had thought it could never happen, became a grand-mother to _____. From that grandson's offspring, Ruth becomes the great-grandmother to what famous king? _____

6. From that same line of ancestry another King is born. We meet His mother, Mary, in the book of Luke as Gabriel announces the news that she will give birth to the Son of God. Although greatly troubled at first (verse 29), Mary's faith is buoyed by her knowledge of the All-Sufficient God.

- Read Luke 1:26-38. What were Gabriel's well-known words to her in Luke 1:37?

- Think of it – the Son of God soon would be nursing at her breast! Read Mary's song of joy in Luke 1:46-55. By what name does she call God in Luke 1:49?

7. Jesus is *El Shaddai* Incarnate. The Gospels portray story after story of the Son of God's generous provision whether it is deserved or not. Here are three of my favorites.

- Read John 6:1-14. How is God's exceedingly abundant provision displayed in this passage?

- Jesus performed many physical healings, but the one that to me shows Almighty God's most tender compassion at a time of high stress is in Luke 22:50-51. What did Jesus do? Why is this healing so surprising?

- Read Luke 23:34. As the Lamb's innocent blood was being poured out, His attention was on the sheep without a shepherd as He prayed, "_____."

- Now it's your turn. Peruse Matthew, Mark, Luke and John or search your memory and jot down three or more examples of *El Shaddai* embodied in Jesus Christ.

8. Paul wrote repeatedly about the God who takes our too little and replaces it with His So Big! What do the following four verses tell us?

- Read II Corinthians 3:5. What does it teach about our adequacy (competence or sufficiency)? Where does it come from?

- Do you feel fragile and ready to break? Read II Corinthians 4:7 to turn that negative into a positive. Where does your power come from? Is there a place in your life where you can use this power right now?

- Philippians 4:13 is a verse that I depend on regularly. It's one that I've passed on to the next generation, one that daughter Emily and I keep passing back and forth. Write out the verse here. For what challenge today will you apply its truth?

- Philippians 4:19 is a whopper of a promise. Where are you coming up short this month? What resources do you need today? Write out the verse (it's worth memorizing) and keep your eyes peeled for *El Shaddai's* liberal supply of all you need.

9. The apostle John walked with Jesus for three years. He watched Him calm a raging storm at sea, cast out demons, heal the sick and raise the dead. He surely trembled as he watched Christ's agonizing death on the cross. Then he beheld the Risen Christ and was an eyewitness to His ascension into heaven. On top of all that, God gave John visions of the heavenly realms, which he recorded in the book of Revelation.

- What does *El Shaddai* tell John in Revelation 1:8?

- Now read out loud and savor Revelation 4:8, realizing as believers we will one day behold this scene with our own eyes. What emotions does this scene stir up in you?

El Shaddai & You

1. Who is *El Shaddai* in your own words?

2. How has acknowledging *El Shaddai* as your personal All-Sufficient One impacted your life?

3. Take some time to write a prayer, poem or Thank You letter to *El Shaddai*.

4. **God Hunt:** Treat yourself to an *El Shaddai* Hunt. Look for signs of Him as the more-than-enough power source in Scripture, in nature, in hymns, in others, in the mirror. Ask Him to open your eyes to notice times when His supply exceeds the demands of your life. Record how you have seen and experienced His more-than-sufficient sufficiency during the week.

I saw *El Shaddai* _____

_____

_____

Date _____

I saw *El Shaddai* _____

_____

Date _____

I saw *El Shaddai* _____
_____
_____

Date _____

5. **A Songfest to *El Shaddai*:** Music can move words of truth from our heads to our hearts. Below are a few songs that highlight *El Shaddai*. Add your favorites, and then grab your instrument of choice or perhaps sing along with a CD or a YouTube video on the Internet. Make a joyful noise to *El Shaddai*!

> *El Shaddai*
> *Jesus Paid It All*
> *He is Able, More Than Able*
> *Mary Did You Know?*
> *All-Sufficient God*

Add any of your favorites:

_____
_____

Notes:

*"The Lord will fight for
you while you keep silent."*

Exodus 14:14 NASB

11

El Gibbor

MIGHTY WARRIOR

I'm Ready to Save Your Day.
May I?

BASIC FACTS

- Both *El* and *Gibbor* mean "mighty." Together, they translate as "Mighty-Mighty God" or "Mighty Warrior God."
- The name is officially announced in Isaiah 9:6.
- The Hebrew word *gibbor* can also be used to describe human strength and might.

EL GIBBOR IN THE BIBLE

1. Moses attests to *El Gibbor's* strength and might as he is prepping the Israelites to enter the Promised Land.

- What does he say in Deuteronomy 10:17?

- From your knowledge of the book of Exodus, list some of the mighty deeds that God had done in Moses' life, beginning with Exodus 2, Moses' miraculous adoption into the house of Pharaoh.

- Now list some of the mighty deeds that *El Gibbor* has done in your own life.

2. The Hebrew word *gibbor* can also refer to a human hero, conqueror or champion – someone with macho and bravado.

- The Philistine's champion, Goliath, had mucho macho. Read about him in I Samuel 17:4-7. What were his heroic characteristics?

- Now consider the contrast between the Philistine champion and God's pick that day for a champion. Who was God's pick and what were his characteristics (I Samuel 17:14-15, 33)?

- In I Samuel 17:45-47, identify the secret of David's victory.

3. Motherhood was a Goliath-size assignment for me, but thanks to the overwhelming challenge, I learned to know God on a first-name basis. When I am weak, then I am strong (in His strength, not mine). Sound familiar? Do you know who wrote this truth? You can find it in II Corinthians 12:10.

- Write out the kingdom principle found in the passage.

- What is your Goliath-size assignment? Are you ready to apply this kingdom principle and allow *El Gibbor* to save your day? Explain how.

4. In writing Psalm 24, David – no longer a shepherd lad – showed that he knew who *El Gibbor* was.

- Read Psalm 24 and write out verse 8. Has there been an instance where you have been especially aware of *El Gibbor's* strength and might?

- Check out other psalms of David, such as 18, 29, 30 and 31. Though *El Gibbor's* name is not mentioned here, these psalms pay tribute to our Mighty Warrior God. Select one and write down phrases that resonate for you.

5. Jeremiah lived during Israel's demise. God's people had broken His heart; His judgment was deserved and imminent. Jeremiah, known as the weeping prophet, experienced pain and persecution yet his spirit was buoyed as he reviewed what he knew about his Mighty Warrior God.

- Read Jeremiah 32:17-22. Where do you see the power and might of *El Gibbor* in these verses?

- What facts about God buoy your spirit when you are feeling down? What truths do you cling to?

6. David's Mighty God had companioned with him when David was a shepherd boy, a soldier, a fugitive running for his life and a king. He knew God to be dependable and awesome.

- Read Psalm 20 and write down what David wants you to know about his *El Gibbor*.

I call Psalm 20 my *El Gibbor* Psalm. It's the one I prayed when overwhelmed with a new set of artificial limbs that didn't work. Falling to the ground with no warning, utterly frustrated and feeling like a failure, I clung to the God who promised to save my day. In the two years I struggled with those lame legs, I enjoyed the increasingly sweet companionship of *El Gibbor*. When the solution finally came, I knew not only Who to thank but Who to hug.

- What about you? What unsolved or unresolved problem threatens to take you down? Listen for *El Gibbor's* offer: "I'm ready to save your day. May I?" Will you let Him? What promise can you cling to from Psalm 20?

7. Like David in Psalm 20, the prophet Isaiah communicates hope. In the midst of Israel's rebellion and judgment, Isaiah's

chapter 9 opens with a holy birth announcement (verses 1-7).

- Write out the four names of the Heralded One that appear in Isaiah 9:6.

- To whom does this passage refer?

8. Think about God's mighty deeds as recorded in the Bible (Old Testament and New Testament). Here are a few that shout *El Gibbor* to me. Add to the list and yes, examples from your own life are welcome!

- Creation (Genesis 1)
- The parting of the Red Sea (Exodus 14)
- Christ calming the raging sea (Matthew 8:23-27)
- Christ on the cross (John 19:16-30)
- The empty tomb (John 20:1-18)
- Your own examples _____

9. *Christ on the cross? The empty tomb?* Yes, Jesus is *El Gibbor* Incarnate. The battle He won on the cross, as evidenced by the empty tomb, is where He stands the strongest as our Mighty Warrior. Most people think of a battered and weakened man hanging silently on a cross, but while He was there, a spiritual battle was raging. Though God does not give us many details, there was some evidence.

- Read Luke 23:44-45 and Matthew 27:50-51, and write down three pieces of evidence to indicate that this was no ordinary crucifixion.

- In chapter 9 of this Bible Study, I elaborated on the reconciliation between sinful man and Holy God that has been made available through Jesus' work on the cross. In most Bible versions, II Corinthians 5:21 says that God the Father made God the Son *to be sin for us.* Read Mark 15:33-34 and record what Jesus said during the intensity of this wondrous transaction.

- When sharing the Gospel with others, my friend Amy often says, "A dead man can't save anyone. But thankfully, Jesus didn't stay dead." Read Luke 24:1-6. What well-known words did the angels say to the women in verse 6a?

- Because our Risen and Mighty Warrior has saved the day, believers not only have eternal life but also His promise for victory for daily living. Read Romans 8:31-37. What does verse 37 say about us?

10. Indeed, God's might exceeds all others. Yet how often does He seem to hold it in check? Do you sometimes secretly think,

Where is El Gibbor when I need Him?

- In what situation has your wait seemed so endless that your patience was (or is) holding on by a mere thread?

- Ultimately we wonder: *Can anything good come out of an endless wait?* Read and write out James 1:2-4.

- According to this passage, what trophies come from a long wait?

- In James and elsewhere, the Bible reminds us not to quit before the happy ending. I love Psalm 71:23 (MSG):

  > *When I open up in song to you,*
  > *I let out lungsful of praise,*
  > *my rescued life a song.*

  What is the song of your rescued life?

El Gibbor & You

1. Who is *El Gibbor* in your own words?

2. How has acknowledging *El Gibbor* as your very own Mighty Warrior impacted your life?

3. Take some time to write a prayer, poem or Thank You letter to *El Gibbor*.

4. **God Hunt:** Treat yourself to an *El Gibbor* Hunt. Look for signs of His mighty presence in Scripture, in nature, in hymns, in others, in the mirror. Invite Him to be your commander-in-chief for the battles of each day. Record each time you see Him save the day during the week.

I saw *El Gibbor* _____

_____

_____

Date _____

I saw *El Gibbor* _____

_____

_____

Date _____

I saw *El Gibbor* _____

_____

_____

Date _____

5. **A Songfest to *El Gibbor*:** Music can move words of truth from our heads to our hearts. Here are a few songs that highlight *El Gibbor*. Add your favorites and then grab your instrument of choice or perhaps sing along with a CD or a YouTube video on the Internet. Make a joyful noise to *El Gibbor*!

> *The Name of the Lord is a Strong Tower*
> *The Warrior is a Child*
> *He is Mighty to Save*
> *King of Glory*
> *Our God*

Add any of your favorites:

_____

_____

Notes:

"He who did not spare His own Son,
but delivered Him up for us all,
how will He not also with Him
freely give us all things?"

Romans 8:32 NASB

12

Jehovah Jireh

THE LORD WILL PROVIDE

In Times of Need, I'm All You Need

BASIC FACTS

- *Jehovah Jireh* means "the LORD will provide."
- The name appears only in Genesis 22:14.
- *Jehovah Jireh* appears only once in the Old Testament and yet is one of the best known of the Hebrew names of God.

JEHOVAH JIREH IN THE BIBLE

1. Mt. Moriah was the supreme test of Abraham's faith in *Jehovah Jireh*. It was there that God asked him to sacrifice something he loved more than life itself. Read the first part of the story in Genesis 22:1-10 and describe:

- God's assignment to Abraham (verses 1-2)

- Abraham's response (verses 3 and 6)

- Abraham's faith attitude (verses 7-8)

If our faith delights the LORD (and it does), then faith coupled with obedience delights Him even more. In ready obedience, Abraham climbed to the top of Mt. Moriah and was ready to plunge the knife into his long-awaited son of promise. Read the rest of the story in Genesis 22:11-14.

- At the crucial moment, what does the LORD say to Abraham (verses 11-12)?

- Then what does He miraculously provide (verse 13)?

- What does Abraham call that place (verse 14)?

2. In Romans 4:18-25, Paul expands on Abraham's uncompromising faith. The New Living Translation describes it this way: *"Abraham never wavered in believing God's promise. In fact, his faith grew stronger, and in this he brought glory to God. He was fully convinced that God is able to do whatever he promises."* (Romans 4:20-21, NLT)

- Surely Abraham's faith exceeds any 1-to-10 faith scale! Like maybe a 50?! What about you? Most of us have some times when our faith is strong and others when it wavers. Use the scale below to indicate your lowest and highest moments of faith.

(1) _____ (10)
Mustard-seed   Mt. Moriah
Faith   Faith

- No matter what your need, God promises to provide "a ram in the thicket." Share a time when your faith was sorely tested but at the crucial moment God's ram appeared. Or, if you are still waiting for that ram, tell about your ongoing faith test.

3. God created each one of us for an intimate relationship with Himself. He longs for us to know Him as the source of all good gifts. "In times of need, I'm all you need," is the beat of His generous heart. Yet God knows our foolish tendency to find joy in the gift rather than the Giver, to treasure our Isaacs more than the Giver of Isaacs.

- Read Genesis 22:12. What did God commend Abraham for? What was Abraham saying to God by his actions?

Lured by the treasures and pleasures of earth, we easily and sometimes unknowingly embrace substitutes for God. The Bible calls these substitutes "idols." An idol is anything that displaces God. God has a cure: "Meet Me on Mt. Moriah."

- What/who have been the idols/Isaacs in your life through the years, be they possessions, positions or special persons? If you are not sure, are you willing to invite God to expose any and all idols in your life?

- Tell how God has pried your fingers loose of your idols. If you are still clinging to them, are you now willing to join Abraham in faithful obedience on Mt. Moriah?

4. God had spared Isaac so as to keep the promise He had made to Abraham in Genesis 17:19: God's covenant nation would come from Isaac. When the time came for Isaac to marry, Abraham sent his servant back to his own country to find a suitable wife (Genesis 24:1-27), and God provided her.

- Read Genesis 24:12-14, and write down the specifics of the servant's prayer of faith.

- Now read Genesis 24:17-19. What did beautiful Rebekah say to the servant?

- What was the servant's response to this specific answer to his prayer (verses 26-27)?

- Has there been a time when you prayed as specifically as that servant and then saw *Jehovah Jireh* provide just as specifically? Explain.

5. Mt. Moriah in the Old Testament is the same geographical site as Mt. Calvary in the New Testament. On Mt. Moriah, a way of escape for Isaac was provided. Two thousand years later on Mt. Calvary, the way of escape for Jesus was withheld.

- Think and write about the similarities between the father/son duo on Mt. Moriah and the Father/Son duo on Mt. Calvary.

- Now contrast what Abraham was willing to do but didn't have to do with what God the Father didn't have to do but did.

6. *Jehovah Jireh* provided a way of escape for Isaac but withheld the way of escape for Jesus. Could it be that on Mt. Calvary He instead provided a way of escape for you and me?

- Read John 3:16. What does God's sacrifice of His Son mean to humanity?

- Now read I Peter 3:18. What does God's sacrifice of His Son mean for you personally?

7. Once you become intimately acquainted with God as your Provider, a couple rounds of *God provides, Jehovah Jireh* may become part of your daily life. Truly, God's gift-giving exceeds our human needs and even our imaginations.

- Read and comment on Romans 8:32.

- List some of the things that He has freely given to you.

8. John, an apostle who witnessed God's Son being given up for us all and then saw the nail-scarred hands of the Risen Savior, testified that in times of need, He is all we need.

- Look up John 1:16. What does your Bible version say about *Jehovah Jireh's* exceedingly great generosity?

I love how the Amplified Bible puts it: *For out of His fullness we all received one grace after another, spiritual blessing upon spiritual blessing, even favor upon favor and gift heaped upon gift.* (John 1:16 AMP)

- Now read Philippians 4:19 and identify the source of

God's infinite storehouse of provisions.

9. If you have doubts about the sufficiency of His storehouse, consider the widow at Zarephath, who told Elijah that she couldn't feed him because she had only a handful of flour and a little oil.

- Read I Kings 17:13-16. How did *Jehovah Jireh* miraculously respond to her need?

- Can you think of other examples from Scripture that demonstrate the abundance of God's storehouse?

- What about you? Do you have a story to tell about a time when God more than provided for your need?

10. As if God's provision wouldn't be enough, there's more. It's called His Presence. He promises to be with us every step of the way. He knows what we'll need, He promises to supply what we need and then He climbs our Mt. Moriahs with us (even carrying us when needed). Jesus Himself is *Jehovah Jireh* past, present and future. Our ram in the thicket.

- Look up, write down and believe Isaiah 43:2. *Jehovah Jireh's* presence is enough.

Jehovah Jireh & You

1. Who is *Jehovah Jireh* in your own words?

2. How has acknowledging *Jehovah Jireh* as the Provider of all of your needs impacted your life?

3. Take some time to write a prayer, poem or Thank You letter to *Jehovah Jireh*.

4. **God Hunt:** Treat yourself to a *Jehovah Jireh* Hunt. Look for signs of His presence in Scripture, in nature, in hymns, in others, in the mirror. Invite Him to open your eyes to see His ongoing provision for all of your needs. Become more daring in your choices to obey, knowing that outside your comfort zone is a good place to meet *Jehovah Jireh*. Record how you have seen and enjoyed His generosity during the week.

I saw *Jehovah Jireh* _____

_____

_____

Date _____

I saw *Jehovah Jireh* _____

_____

_____

Date _____

I saw *Jehovah Jireh* _____

_____

_____

Date _____

5. **A Songfest to *Jehovah Jireh*:** Music can move words of truth from our heads to our hearts. Here are a few songs that highlight *Jehovah Jireh*. Add your favorites and then grab your instrument of choice or perhaps sing along with a CD or a YouTube video on the Internet. Make a joyful noise to *Jehovah Jireh*!

He Giveth More Grace
God Provides
Great is Thy Faithfulness
God Will Take Care of You
I Will Sing of the Mercies

Add any of your favorites:

_____

_____

Notes:

_____

_____

_____

_____

_____

_____

_____

_____

_____

_____

_____

_____

_____

_____

_____

_____

_____

_____

_____

_____

_____

_____

_____

"And Mary said,
'Behold, the bondslave of the Lord;
may it be done to me according
to your word.'"

Luke 1:38a NASB

13

Adonai

LORD AND MASTER

*The God Who Patiently Awaits
the Honor He is Due*

BASIC FACTS

- *Adonai* means "Lord and Master."
- *Adonai* is also translated as "Sovereign" in some Bibles; *Adonai Jehovah*: Sovereign LORD.
- The name *Adonai*, which is used hundreds of times in the Old Testament, appears first in Genesis 15.
- English Bibles represent *Adonai* as Lord, not to be confused with the same word capitalized, LORD, referring to *Jehovah*.

ADONAI IN THE BIBLE

1. In Genesis 15, God appeared to Abram in a vision to announce His covenant with Abram and His plan for his life.

- Read Genesis 15:2 and write the name of God used by Abram when he responded.

The Names of God Bible says Abram called Him "*Adonai Jehovah,*" thus acknowledging God as the Sovereign LORD. Abram had questions (verses 3-4), but ultimately he trusted God. And though God did not reveal every detail of His plan, God's answers (verses 4-5) were enough for Abram at that time.

- Read and write out Genesis 15:6, which documents the faith transaction between Abram and *Adonai*. What did Abram do, and what did God do in response?

- Do you have questions about an uncertain future? What can you do right now to entrust the outcome to *Adonai*?

2. Scripture records Moses', Gideon's and Jeremiah's submission to God as each was given a Herculean assignment. Interestingly, each declaration of submission was accompanied by an admission of inadequacy.

- What does Moses say in Exodus 4:10-13?

- What does Gideon say in Judges 6:15?

- What does Jeremiah say in Jeremiah 1:6?

Each man expressed weakness as he faced what seemed impossible. Could it be that our admission of weakness is not only okay but essential before we can know God as our personal *Adonai*? Could it be that inadequacy moves us from self-reliance to God-reliance?

- Give an example of how your personal sense of inadequacy proved to be a blessing in disguise. Did God show up? What happened next?

3. *Adonai* showed up again and again for the prophets of old, breathing strength and hope into their desperate situations as they submitted to His Lordship and experienced the joy of His presence.

- Read Habakkuk 3:17. Describe the conditions that this prophet faced.

- What choice does Habakkuk make in verse 18?

In verse 19, Habakkuk addresses God as *Jehovah Adonai*, acknowledging Him as his own Lord and Master. I penned my initials by that verse almost 50 years ago. When I was a new Christian and a scared-to-death college student during final exam week, Habakkuk's victory cry instantly became mine. I love the Amplified version, which reads: "*The Lord God is my*

Strength, my personal bravery, and my invincible army; He makes my feet like hinds' feet and will make me to walk [not to stand still in terror, but to walk] and make [spiritual] progress upon my high places [of trouble, suffering, or responsibility]!" (Habakkuk 3:19 AMP)

- Read the verse in your own Bible and write what your version says. In what fearsome situation do you need *Adonai's* strength and presence to accomplish the impossible?

4. Forty years after the fact I can still hear my Adult Sunday School teacher Bob Roe admonishing a roomful of seasoned Christians to become Jesus Christ's *doulos* (Greek for bond-servant). I didn't get it then, but I hear it loud and clear now: "Jesus died in your place and He rose to give you eternal life, yes, but also life to the full now. Embrace Him as your *Adonai*. Bow to Jesus Christ as Lord and Master."

- Thanks to that Sunday School teacher, the word *doulos* became burned into my memory; my ears perk up at its mention. What do you notice about the salutations in the following New Testament epistles of Paul?
  ◦ Romans 1:1
  ◦ Philippians 1:1
  ◦ Titus 1:1

- Now examine II Peter 1:1 and Revelation 1:1, written by Peter and John, respectively. How do these men identify themselves?

- Two surprising proponents to servanthood are James and Jude, the two skeptical brothers of Jesus who changed their tune after His resurrection. Look up James 1:1 and Jude 1:1 and record what each man called himself.

- Then there was the virgin peasant girl, who was told by the angel Gabriel that she would bear the Son of God. Look up Luke 1:38 and comment on Mary's response to such shocking news.

5. A *doulos*, or bondservant, is one whose will is swallowed up in the will of another; one who serves another even if it costs him his life.

- Study Philippians 2:5-8. Whom is Paul talking about? What does this Bondservant give up?

- According to Philippians 2:9-11, what is the reward of His obedient sacrifice?

- Write out the words of Philippians 2:10a, words that confirm the Lordship of *Adonai* Incarnate.

6. In I Corinthians 6:19b-20a, the apostle Paul says "you are not your own; you were bought with a price." Jesus bought you with His sacrifice; He earned the right to own you. When you invite Him into your heart, you become His. But the God who patiently awaits the honor He is due does not force His Lordship; He waits for you to ask Him be your *Adonai*.

- Where are you with letting God be your Boss 24/7? Are you willing to be God's bondservant, with your will swallowed up in His? Explain your answer.

7. The concept of being a bondservant may be totally new to you. You may be asking, "How do I do it?"

- Paul gives part of the answer in Romans 12:1. Read the verse and consider what presenting your body as a living sacrifice means to you. Give examples of how you might do this throughout the day.

- Now read Romans 12:2. How does turning from the world's view of things and renewing your mind (with God's thoughts from Scripture) help you become a faithful *doulos*?

- In John 15:4-5, Jesus gives the rest of the answer. Read and comment on His words.

8. Are you ready to become *Adonai's doulos*? It doesn't mean you rev up your determination to be the best *doulos* ever. The truth is, when we succeed at anything in our own strength, we fail. Becoming His bondservant means: *I acknowledge that I am owned by God. I surrender my rights to Him as a loving act of worship.*

- If that is the desire of your heart, tell God you are ready to give Him the honor He is due. Then remember the following things:
  - It's a daily commitment, not a one-time thing.
  - It means beginning each day with, "Lord, what are we going to do together today?"
  - It means asking Him throughout the day, "Is this Your will, my Lord?"

- When and how do you plan on implementing this surrendered heart attitude?

9. The Lord knows that our greatest joy is tucked into submission and obedience. He also knows that surrendering our will does not come easy. Even as an amputee I have a history of digging in my heels. That's why I love Psalm 119:32, my "SOS

verse" when my resistance rages. In the Amplified Bible it says, "*I will (not merely walk, but) run the way of Your commandments, when You give me a heart that is willing.*" (Psalm 119:32 AMP)

- Look up the verse in your own Bible and put your initials by it if you want God to give you a heart that is willing. Write your personal prayer of submission to His Lordship here.

10. Write your response to the following quote. Does it convey the desire of your heart? "When we allow God's sovereignty in our lives, our captivity ends."

Adonai & You

1. Who is *Adonai* in your own words?

2. How has acknowledging *Adonai* as your personal Lord and Master impacted your life?

3. Take some time to write a prayer, poem or Thank You letter to *Adonai*.

4. **God Hunt:** Treat yourself to an *Adonai* Hunt. Look for signs of His presence in Scripture, in nature, in hymns, in others, in the mirror. Invite Him to be Lord over you as you bow to His perfect will. Record how you have seen him reward your submission with His mighty power to accomplish the impossible during the week.

I saw *Adonai* _____

_____

_____

Date _____

I saw *Adonai* _____

_____

_____

Date _____

I saw *Adonai* _____

_____

_____

Date _____

5. **A Songfest to *Adonai*:** Music can move words of truth from our heads to our hearts. Here are a few songs that highlight *Adonai*. Add your favorites and then grab your instrument of choice or perhaps sing along with a CD or a YouTube video on the Internet. Make a joyful noise to *Adonai*!

I Surrender All

He is Lord

Christ the Lord is Risen Today

Jesus Take the Wheel

My Adonai

Have Thine Own Way, Lord

Add any of your favorites:

_____

_____

Notes:

_____
_____
_____
_____
_____
_____
_____
_____
_____
_____
_____
_____
_____
_____
_____
_____
_____
_____
_____
_____
_____
_____
_____

"He brought me up out of the pit of
destruction, out of the miry clay,
And He set my feet upon a rock
making my footsteps firm."

Psalm 40:2 NASB

14

Adonai Tsuri

THE LORD MY ROCK
The Rock-Solid God Who Makes Us Unshakeable

BASIC FACTS

- *Adonai Tsuri* means "the Lord my Rock."
- In the Old Testament we learn about God the Rock through Moses, Hannah, David, Joshua and Samuel.
- Jesus is the ultimate spiritual Rock for those who believe.

ADONAI TSURI IN THE BIBLE

1. Not long after leaving Egypt, Moses was faced with the challenge and responsibility of quenching the thirst of three-million-plus fractious Israelites.

- Read Exodus 17:1-7. Complete the following sentences:

    As the children of Israel were suffering from
    _____, God instructed Moses
    to strike the _____.
    When Moses did so, _____
    flowed in abundance.

In Numbers 20:2-12, another water crisis occurs. This time Moses is told to do something different.

- Take careful note of God's instruction in verse 8. How did it differ from what He said in Exodus?

- Now describe Moses' actions in verses 9-11. Did he obey?

- Moses faced serious consequences for his actions. Read Numbers 20:12 and Deuteronomy 34:1-5. What did his disobedience cost him?

2. All of us have disobeyed God's instructions. Thankfully, God's mercy and love remains rock-solid even when we fail.

- Read Psalm 95:1. To whom does the psalmist invite us to sing and shout for joy?

- It is evident from his writings that Moses knew God as his personal Rock. Read his song in Deuteronomy 32 and count the number of references to the Rock.

- Write out Moses' conclusion about *Adonai Tsuri* in Deuteronomy 32:4.

3. Another individual who knew God as the Rock-Solid One who made her unshakeable was Hannah. In I Samuel, chapter 1 we learn of her travail over her barrenness and her heartbroken prayer for a child. Chapter 2 contains her song of thanksgiving after she conceives and gives birth to Samuel.

- How does she refer to God in I Samuel 2:2?

- Have you ever beseeched the Lord with that much agony and then seen Him come through in rock-solid faithfulness to answer your prayer? Tell about that time.

4. The shepherd-king David's life story is filled with references to God his Rock.

- Read his song of deliverance in II Samuel 22 and identify his three references to the Rock.

- David exalts *Adonai Tsuri* as his refuge, strength and fortress in many of his psalms. Take note of the common word in the following examples. Then add your own favorite "God Is My Rock" verse from a psalm.
  - Psalm 18:2 (a favorite of my editor's)
  - Psalm 61:2 (a favorite of my dad's)
  - Psalm 144:1-2 (a favorite of mine)
  - Your favorite: _____

5. After Moses' death, Joshua was chosen to lead God's people into the Promised Land. To do so, they had to cross the Jordan River, which was running at flood stage.

- Read Joshua 3:15-17. By what mighty act did God enable the Israelites to cross over?

- In Joshua 4:1-2, the Lord gives special instructions. What were they?

- Record the reason given by Joshua for those instructions (verses 6-7).

- How were these remembrance stones to be used in the future (verses 21-24)?

6. The Israelites' twelve stones by the Jordan would remind them and future generations that their Rock-Solid God made them unshakeable even at the shores of a raging river. Another stone of remembrance for them is introduced in I Samuel 7, commemorating God's deliverance from the Philistines.

- Read I Samuel 7:12. What did Samuel call the stone he set in their place of victory? Why? What does the name mean (read your Bible's footnote)?

My friend Bob Bonner has some great advice about memorial stones in our own lives.

> Setting up personal memorials of God's faithfulness in one's life can be good. They can become places of worship and praise to God, places to express a thankful heart. They can be used to point others to the personal truth that your God reigns!
>
> What would be some personal memorials from your walk that you can point to as a testimony of praise to God's faithfulness in your life? [16]

- What is your answer to Bob's question?

- What are some practical ways you can incorporate memorial stones into your collection of treasures to be passed on to the next generation?

7. Jesus in the New Testament was the embodiment of *Adonai Tsuri* in the Old Testament.

- What does He say about Himself in Matthew 21:42?

- What does Peter say about Him in I Peter 2:4-8?

8. Paul makes the connection between Jesus the Source of Living Water in the New Testament and Moses' water source in the Old Testament. Read I Corinthians 10:4. What does this verse say about Jesus Christ?

In his *Complete Bible Commentary*, Matthew Henry summarizes Christ's role as our Rock as follows:

> Nothing will supply the needs, and satisfy the desires of a soul, but water out of this rock (Jesus Christ), this fountain opened. The pleasures of sense are puddle-water; spiritual delights are rock-water, so pure, so refreshing—rivers of pleasure.[17]

As the Israelites were satisfied by water from the rock in the wilderness, so we are spiritually satisfied by Jesus as we drink from His fountain. The choice is before us: do we want puddle-water or rock-water?

- What's the puddle-water in your own life from which you are tempted to drink? Have you ever found that water to be truly satisfying in the long run?

- In contrast, in what ways have you experienced the rivers of pleasure that come from the rock-water of Jesus?

9. Anyone remember the Sunday School song, "The Wise Man Built His House Upon a Rock"? The song is based on Matthew 7:24-27, which contains Christ's parable about building our lives on either rock or sand.

- Read the parable to refresh your memory. According to verse 24, how do you build your life on rock? Give some examples of how that looks in your life.

- Give a specific example of a time when you built your life on rock and elaborate on the consequences.

- Now read verse 26. How does a sand-built life come about? Tell about a time when you built your life on the sand. Was the outcome good or bad?

10. In one of his psalms, David traces the believer's progression from shifting sands to the Rock-Solid God who makes us unshakeable.

- Read Psalm 40:1-3. What is the progression?
  From _____ (verse 2a)
  to _____ (verse 2b)
  to _____ (verse 3)

- Do these verses describe you? How and when has the Rock pulled you out of the pit?

- Verse 3b teaches that when the *Adonai Tsuri* saves us, our lives become a testimony. Who sees and hears your testimony? Has anyone come to know our Rock-Solid God because of your song of faith?

Adonai Tsuri & You

<hr/>

1. Who is *Adonai Tsuri* in your own words?

2. How has acknowledging *Adonai Tsuri* as your personal Rock impacted your life?

3. Take some time to write a prayer, poem or Thank You letter to *Adonai Tsuri*.

4. **God Hunt:** Treat yourself to an *Adonai Tsuri* Hunt. Look for signs of His presence in Scripture, in nature, in hymns, in others, in the mirror. Ask Him to open your eyes to His rock-solid stability and safety. Look for creative ways to memorialize His presence. Record how you have seen and enjoyed His unshakeable strength during the week.

I saw *Adonai Tsuri* _____

_____

_____

Date _____

I saw *Adonai Tsuri* _____

_____

_____

Date _____

I saw *Adonai Tsuri* _____

_____

_____

Date _____

5. **A Songfest to *Adonai Tsuri*:** Music can move words of truth from our heads to our hearts. Here are a few songs that highlight *Adonai Tsuri*. Add your favorites and then grab your instrument of choice or perhaps sing along with a CD or a YouTube video on the Internet. Make a joyful noise to *Adonai Tsuri*!

Rock of Ages
The Solid Rock
Beneath the Cross of Jesus
Rock of My Salvation
Firm Foundation
The Wise Man Built His House Upon the Rock

Add any of your favorites:

_____

_____

Notes:

". . . for by His wounds
you were healed."

1 Peter 2:24b NASB

15

Jehovah Rapha

THE GOD WHO HEALS

*The Healer God Who Makes
All Suffering Worth It*

BASIC FACTS

- *Jehovah Rapha* means "the LORD who heals."
- The name *Jehovah Rapha* appears only in Exodus 15:26, but His healing grace permeates Scripture.
- Jesus was *Jehovah Rapha* Incarnate, as evidenced by His miraculous healings throughout the Gospels.
- Jesus ultimately came to earth to heal our sin-sick souls.

JEHOVAH RAPHA IN THE BIBLE

1. After the miraculous crossing of the Red Sea, Moses and the newly freed Israelites were settling into their new normal in the desert when confronted with undrinkable water.

- Read Exodus 15:22-26. What was God's solution to the bitter-water problem?

- What did God promise? Was it unconditional?

- By what name did God call Himself in the last part of verse 26?

2. An Israelite slave girl so trusted in the healing power of *Jehovah Rapha* that she dared suggest to Naaman's wife that Naaman go to the Lord's prophet Elisha to be healed of his leprosy. Look up the story in II Kings 5:1-19.

- Rather than meet Naaman himself, Elisha sent a messenger with God's instructions for Naaman. What did God say Naaman must do to be healed (verse 10)?

- Why did Naaman balk? What had he expected (5:11-12)?

- What happened when his servants convinced him to obey (verse 14)?

- Has there been a time when you balked at God's clear instruction from His word only to find healing (maybe spiritual rather than physical) when you finally obeyed?

3. Jeremiah, the weeping prophet, was well aware of humanity's need for healing.

- Comment on the progression of his emotions and faith from his cry in Jeremiah 8:21-22 to his prayer in Jeremiah 17:14.

- What is the LORD's promise in Jeremiah 30:17?

4. Hosea was a prophet sent to the Israelites to rebuke their faithlessness in their covenant with God.

- Look up and record Hosea's verse about God the Healer in Hosea 6:1. What does the verse mean?

- Does this fit into your concept of a good God? Does it help to remember that He is the Healer God who makes all suffering worth it?

- Look up Psalm 119:71 in your favorite translation(s). Are you able to add your AMEN to the verse?

- For what affliction can you thank God? For what affliction do you need to ask Him to give you a thankful heart?

5. Out of the Bible's 150 psalms, there is one to fit each type

human ailment, be it physical, mental, emotional or spiritual.

- What is your favorite psalm? Why?

- Read Psalm 103:1-5. What types of healing are addressed? Which verses do you need to claim right now? (These are good verses to memorize for any future appointments with health crises.)

- How tenderly *Jehovah Rapha* cares for our wounds of body, soul and spirit. What does Psalm 147:3 tell us about our Great Physician's care?

- No physician can heal us until we go to him or her. Likewise, we must go to *Jehovah Rapha* and hand over the broken pieces and broken places of our lives. Can you share a personal example of handing your pain over to God and watching as He restored you physically, emotionally or spiritually?

6. Jesus Christ, God Incarnate, embodies all of the Old Testament names of God, including *Jehovah Rapha*. To say Jesus was a healer is an understatement: The four Gospels record numerous healings, and still not every healing He performed has been recorded (see John 21:25). Is there a certain one that

stands out in your memory? My favorite occurred in John chapter 9.

- What did Jesus' disciples want to know when they saw the blind man (verse 1)?

- Write down Jesus' answer from verse 3, and remember: that's the perspective of our healer God who makes all suffering worth it toward broken people like you and me.

- Explain how Jesus' perspective changes your attitude toward a visible or invisible disability in yourself or others.

- God's surprise is that He is capable of using a broken family member to demonstrate who He really is – a source of unexplainable wholeness and holiness. How have you seen this happen in your own circle of family or friends?

7. Leave it to God to elevate brokenness to a position of strength and healing. The apostle Paul experienced this conundrum himself, as he explained in II Corinthians 12:7-10.

- What did Paul ask of God (verses 7-8)?

- How did Jesus answer (verse 9a)?

- What was Paul's glorious conclusion for himself and for us (verses 9b-10)?

- How has *Jehovah Rapha's* power been made perfect in your weakness? How has He made suffering worth it?

8. It's important to have clarity about why Jesus Christ came to earth. Yes, He was a great teacher; yes, He lived a pure and perfect life worth imitating. But far more than that, He came as *Jehovah Rapha*, the only One with a cure for humanity's sin-sick souls.

- Read Isaiah 53:4-5, a prophetic passage that describes the crucifixion of the coming Messiah. From verse 5, write the words and phrases that indicate how sinners are healed and given peace through Him.

- Now read I Peter 2:24. Again, write the words and phrases that convey what Jesus did so that we can be spiritually healed.

9. By His stripes (or wounds) we are healed. The soldier's

spear brought forth water and blood, which Christ poured out willingly to quench our thirst and wash us white as snow. Indeed, Christ's wounds have great healing power.

- Read about Jesus' post-resurrection interaction with his disciple Thomas in John 20:24-29. What did Thomas insist on seeing and touching?

- What moved him from unbelief to belief?

- Write out his declaration of faith.

Brennan Manning says, "Doubting Thomas discovered his God in the wounds of Jesus."[18] Wounds, both *Jehovah Rapha's* and ours, set the stage for a meeting and dialogue between God and broken humanity.

- What about you? Have your wounds met His? Write what happened in the form of a prayer of thanksgiving to the God Who Heals.

1. Who is *Jehovah Rapha* in your own words?

2. How has acknowledging *Jehovah Rapha* as your personal Healer God impacted your life?

3. Take some time to write a prayer, poem or Thank You letter to *Jehovah Rapha.*

4. **God Hunt:** Treat yourself to *Jehovah Rapha* Hunt. Look for signs of His presence in Scripture, in nature, in hymns, in others, in the mirror. Be alert to His healing touch in your physical, emotional and spiritual weaknesses. Invite Him to reveal Himself in new ways in your suffering. Record how you have seen Him make it all worth it during the week.

I saw *Jehovah Rapha* _____

_____

_____

Date _____

I saw *Jehovah Rapha* _____

_____

_____

Date _____

I saw *Jehovah Rapha* _____

_____

_____

Date _____

5. **A Songfest to *Jehovah Rapha*:** Music can move words of truth from our heads to our hearts. Here are a few songs that highlight *Jehovah Rapha*. Add your favorites and then grab your instrument of choice or perhaps sing along with a CD or a YouTube video on the Internet. Make a joyful noise to *Jehovah Rapha*!

There is a Balm in Gilead
By His Wounds
He Touched Me
Jesus, Your Name is Power
Jesus Heals

Add any of your favorites:

_____

_____

Notes:

"*Now may the Lord of
peace Himself continually grant
you peace in every circumstance.
The Lord be with you all!*"

II Thessalonians 3:16 NASB

16

Jehovah Shalom

THE LORD IS PEACE

*The God Who Calms Our
Storms Inside and Out*

BASIC FACTS

- *Jehovah Shalom* means "the LORD is peace."
- The name appears only in the book of Judges.
- Though the name appears only once, God offers His peace throughout the Bible to all who believe.
- *Jehovah Shalom's* ultimate peace is ours through Jesus.

JEHOVAH SHALOM IN THE BIBLE

1. The book of Judges portrays a dark age in the history of God's people, the Israelites. Joshua, their leader after Moses, had died. Since they had no earthly leader, *"Everyone did what was right in his own eyes."* (Judges 17:6, 21:25 NASB). In that context, *Jehovah Shalom* comes a-callin' on Gideon, who was hiding out from the Midianites for fear of his life. Gideon's amazing story is recorded in Judges 6:11–8:35.

- Read about Gideon's encounter with *Jehovah Shalom* in

Judges 6:11-24. What did the angel of the LORD call Gideon (verse 12)? Why does that title make one chuckle?

• Gideon refers to God with what name in verse 24?

2. The truth is, each one of us is a Scaredy Cat Gideon needing a house call from *Jehovah Shalom*. Thankfully, we can encounter Him in the Word of God. No ordinary book, it contains truths that equip, empower and give peace to those who believe.

• To me, a believer's best remedy for a sleepless night is Psalm 23. Why waste time counting sheep when you can get peace from the Shepherd? Read the familiar psalm and write down verses that speak peace to your heart.

3. My friend Ginny says that her secret to peace is tucked in Psalm 46:10. Her job is not to fret, panic or take charge but to be still and know that God is God. Those few words transform her from a Scaredy Cat to a Valiant Warrior because, like Gideon, she knows *Jehovah Shalom* has shown up.

• Read Ginny's Peace Psalm 46 and discover the God-bookends in verses 1 and 11. What words in those bookends would calm you in a storm?

- Do you have a personal Peace Psalm? Which one (or ones) do you read regularly to remind you of the LORD your Peace?

4. *Jehovah Shalom* knows that we humans are always in need of peace. And He is always willing to give it to those who ask.

- Read Numbers 6:22-27, the priestly blessing God instructed Moses to teach Aaron and his sons. I can still hear my minister father ending his Sunday service with this soothing benediction. What does verse 26 say?

- Not only does God want to give us peace, He also wants us to know it is always there for us. Look up Isaiah 54:10 and comment on God's promise to His own.

5. The prophet Isaiah wrote during the stormy period when the Assyrian empire was expanding and Israel was declining. Isaiah 26 was a song of praise in the storm; verse 3 contains a path to peace for believers.

- Write out the verse and explain how God rewards those who trust in Him.

The Amplified Bible's rendering perhaps brings more clarity:

"You will guard him and keep him in perfect and constant peace whose mind [both its inclination and its character] is stayed on You, because he commits himself to You, leans on You, and hopes confidently in You." (Isaiah 26:3 AMP)

- How are you doing in this trusting God category? And what does your peace barometer read right now?

6. Ultimately, true peace begins with God and is found only in the person of Jesus Christ, who is the way, the truth and the life. The prophet Isaiah heralds him – *Jehovah Shalom* Incarnate – 700 years before His birth.

- Read Isaiah 9:6 and record the four titles given to the coming Christ.

- That He came to bring peace was confirmed by his heavenly birth announcement. Read Luke 2:14 and record the familiar Christmas words.

- What does the Prince of Peace promise to His followers, as recorded in John 14:27?

7. The peace of God is offered to everyone, but it is a gift that must be received under His terms. A simple path to under-

standing those terms is known as The Romans Road.

- Read the following verses in order, and jot down a brief paraphrase of each passage. If you have yet to make your peace with God, ask Him to help you open your heart to Him as you read.
  ◦ Romans 3:23
  ◦ Romans 6:23
  ◦ Romans 5:8
  ◦ Romans 10:9-10 and 13

- The final verse of The Romans Road is chapter 5, verse 1. What does that verse say we have when we have placed our faith in Jesus Christ?

8. Yet even those of us who are already walking the Peace Path with Jesus find there are thieves ever at the ready to steal our inner calm. Worry is one of the biggest crooks out there.

- Read what Jesus has to say about our worry in Matthew 6:25-34. According to verse 33, what is His ultimate cure?

- Knowing the cure doesn't automatically erase our anxiety, however. What does Paul advise us to do in Philippians 4:4-6? Write down his step-by-step formula for peace (which, amazingly, was written while in prison).

- When we follow Paul's formula, what will the outcome be, according to Philippians 4:7?

- When have you personally experienced the outcome described after following the formula?

9. As a new Christian, I often relied on God's promise recorded by Peter in I Peter 5:7. In the midst of stress, I'd remind myself to "I Peter 5:7" my cares.

- Read the verse and comment on how easy or difficult it is for you to apply in your own life.

- Perhaps it would be easier for us to do what verse 7 says if we add verse 6 to the process as well. Go back and read I Peter 5:6. What heart attitude is necessary?

10. What cares would you love to have out of your hands right now? The God who calms our storms inside and out invites you to hand them over so that you can receive what is yours in Christ.

- Read John 16:33. What does Jesus say is yours?

Now claim as your own this invitation from the Peace-giver:
(author's paraphrase of Psalm 16:33)

My Beloved –
In Me you may have peace, serenity and harmony.
In the world you will have disappointment,
misery, adversity. But let Me be your courage.
I have overcome, defeated and risen above the world –
And so will you.

Love, Your Prince of Peace

- Respond to this "love note" with a love letter of your own. Tell *Jehovah Shalom* about your storms, and let Him know you are ready to let Him calm them.

Jehovah Shalom & You

—•◦•—

1. Who is *Jehovah Shalom* in your own words?

2. How has acknowledging *Jehovah Shalom* as your personal Prince of Peace impacted your life?

3. Take some time to write a prayer, poem or Thank You letter to *Jehovah Shalom*.

4. **God Hunt:** Treat yourself to a *Jehovah Shalom* Hunt. Pursue His peace in Scripture, in nature, in hymns, in others, in the mirror. Invite Him to calm your internal and external storms with His peace that passes all understanding. Invite Him to increase your awareness of personal and interpersonal distress so you can enlist His help. Record how you have enjoyed His peace during the week.

I saw *Jehovah Shalom* _____

_____

_____

Date _____

I saw *Jehovah Shalom* _____

_____

_____

Date _____

I saw *Jehovah Shalom* _____

_____

_____

Date _____

5. **A Songfest to *Jehovah Shalom*:** Music can move words of truth from our heads to our hearts. Here are a few songs that highlight *Jehovah Shalom*. Add your favorites and then grab your instrument of choice or perhaps sing along with a CD or a YouTube video on the Internet. Make a joyful noise to *Jehovah Shalom*!

Peace Perfect Peace
It is Well with My Soul
I've Got Peace Like a River
Like a River Glorious
He is Our Peace
He Already Sees
Praise You in the Storm

Add any of your favorites:

_____

_____

Notes:

"Now may the God of peace Himself sanctify you entirely. . . . Faithful is He who calls you, and He also will bring it to pass."

I Thessalonians 5:23a-24 NASB

17

Jehovah Mekoddishkem

THE LORD WHO SANCTIFIES

*The Only One Who Can Perfect
Us into a Masterpiece*

BASIC FACTS

- *Jehovah Mekoddishkem* means "the LORD who sanctifies."
- The Hebrew name appears in the book of Leviticus.
- The English word *sanctification* comes from the Latin *santificatio*, meaning "the process of making holy, consecrated."
- The spiritual process of sanctification, though a shared responsibility between God and us, is a gift from God. Only He can do the true work of perfecting us.

JEHOVAH MEKODDISHKEM IN THE BIBLE

1. Understanding the LORD who sanctifies and the process of sanctification begins with understanding God's holiness.

  - Read Isaiah 6:1-3, the account of the time when the prophet Isaiah saw the LORD sitting on a throne. Write down what the seraphims were calling to one another.

- Compare Isaiah's vision with what John reported in Revelation 4:8. Write down what the four living creatures in that vision never stopped saying.

2. Apart from the LORD, there is no holiness. To emphasize how important it is that we grasp God's holiness, R.C. Sproul makes this comment:

> The Bible says that God is holy, holy, holy. Not that He is merely holy, or even holy, holy. He is holy, holy, holy. The Bible never says that God is love, love, love, or mercy, mercy, mercy, or wrath, wrath, wrath, or justice, justice, justice. It does say that He is holy, holy, holy, the whole earth is full of His glory.[19]

- Look up the word *holy* in a Bible dictionary as well as a regular one and then write your own definition here.

- Tell of a time in your public worship, private prayer or personal Bible reading when your awareness of God's holiness impacted you deeply.

3. When the Holy God identifies Himself to Moses as *Jehovah Mekoddishkem* in Leviticus 20:7-8, He also issues a command.

• What does He say His people must do (verse 7a, 8a)?

At the same time, He hints at the fact that we can only obey this command in His power. The Message translation of the passage says: *"Set yourselves apart for a holy life. Live a holy life, because I am* God*, your God. Do what I tell you; live the way I tell you. I am the* God *who makes you holy."* (Leviticus 20:7-8 MSG)

• According to this, what is God's part in your holiness?

• What is your part?

• To see more clearly how to do your part, read James 1:22. What two things does James say you must do?

4. The sanctification of believers – past, present and future – was on Jesus' heart during the Last Supper with His disciples.

• What did He pray in John 17:17 and 19?

• According to His prayer, by what are we sanctified?

5. But what exactly is sanctification? My pastor, Ray Stedman, explained it in a sermon almost 40 years ago and I've never forgotten it:

> Sanctification is the process by which the inner worth which God imparts to our human spirit by faith in Christ begins to work itself out into our conduct. We actually begin to change. We begin to be like what we actually are. Therefore, our attitudes change, and our actions change, and our habits begin to change, and we stop certain things and begin others. Our whole demeanor is different; we become much more gracious, happy, wholesome persons. That is called sanctification.[20]

- To see how God is working out the sanctification process in your life, give one example of how He has changed:
  ◦ Your desires
  ◦ Your attitude
  ◦ Your actions and habits
  ◦ Your self-worth
  ◦ Your ability to love and forgive
  ◦ Your ability to believe God is good when it doesn't feel that way

6. If we are not careful, we may begin to think we can achieve sanctification on our own or earn it by our merit. But God's

Word makes it clear that sanctification – just like salvation – is God's gift.

- Read Ephesians 1:4. When did the process of your holiness begin?

When we receive Jesus as our own personal Savior, God says that Jesus' righteousness becomes ours. (See II Corinthians 5:21 and chapter 9 in this Bible Study.) We are justified before our Holy God and reconciled with Him. Only then can His work of sanctifying us begin.

- Read II Corinthians 5:17-18a. What does Paul call anyone who has received Christ? Who does this come from?

Receiving God the Son also means receiving God the Holy Spirit, who indwells us and works in us to perfect us into His masterpiece.

- The apostle Paul confirms this in I Corinthians 3:16. What does he say?

7. The apostle Peter maps out the road to holiness in II Peter 1:2-9. I can remember a time in my life when I plodded step by step through the sequence, checking off where I was and what I had yet to learn from *Jehovah Mekoddishkem*. Study the fol-

lowing paraphrase from The Living Bible.

> *Do you want more and more of God's kind-ness and peace? Then learn to know Him bet-ter and better. For as you know him better, he will give you through his great power every-thing you need for living a good life. He even shares his own glory and goodness with us. And by that same mighty power He has given us all the other rich and wonderful blessings he promised: for instance, the promise to save us from the lust and rottenness all around us, and to give us his own character.*
>
> *But to obtain these gifts, you need more than faith. You must also work hard to be good and even that is not enough. For then you must learn to know God better and discover what he wants you to do. Next learn to put aside your own desires so that you will become pa-tient and godly, gladly letting God have his way with you. This will make possible the next step, which is for you to enjoy other peo-ple and to like them and finally you will grow to love them deeply. The more you go on in this way, the more you will grow strong spir-itually and become fruitful and useful to the Lord Jesus Christ. But anyone who fails to go after these additions to faith is blind indeed*

or at least very shortsighted and has forgot-
ten that God delivered him from the old life of
sin so that now he can live a strong, good life
for the Lord. (II Peter 1:2-9 TLB)

- Where you are in the process of
  - knowing Him better and better?
  - experiencing His mighty power?
  - seeing His character growing in you?
  - setting aside your desires to let God have His way?
  - enjoying, liking and loving others?
  - growing strong spiritually?
  - becoming fruitful and useful to Jesus?

8. How wonderful that we do not walk that road of holiness alone! *Jehovah Mekoddishkem* is right there with us. Our job is to fill ourselves with His Word and surrender ourselves to the Holy Spirit's work in us. His job is to create the masterpiece He saw before the beginning of time.

- Read Paul's inspired words in Romans 8:29. Don't get hung up on the words *foreknew* and *predestined*; focus instead on who Paul says we will be like. Write that part of the verse here.

Me? The image of His Son? Yes, that is the crux of sanctification. And there's more: As He conforms us to His likeness, He wants to use our sanctified lives to touch the lives of others.

- Read Ephesians 2:10. What does the verse say you are? What does it say you were created for?

Study The Message's rendering of I Peter 2:9-10: "*But you are the ones chosen by God, chosen for the high calling of priestly work, chosen to be a holy people, God's instruments to do his work and speak out for him, to tell others of the night-and-day difference he made for you—from nothing to something, from rejected to accepted.*" (MSG)

- What work does God have in mind for every believer?

- What night-and-day difference has He made in your life? Who have you told?

- Think of at least one area where He has moved you from:
  ○ nothing to something
  ○ rejected to accepted

9. Right about now God's enemy and ours – Satan, the father of lies – may jump in and tell you that you are a nothing, a reject. Don't let him get a foothold! Remind yourself that the Lord who sanctifies will not leave you unfinished.

- Read the following verses and personalize them by replacing the pronouns with your name.
  - Philippians 1:6 (Does it say He *might* or He *will*?)
  - Jude 24-25 (How is He going to present you?)

Your best weapon of defense against Satan the Shamer is the same one Jesus used when tempted in the wilderness.

- Read Matthew 4, verses 4, 7 and 10. What three words did Jesus say in each instance?

If defeating the devil with God's Word was good enough for Jesus, it's certainly good enough for us! Over the years, I have filled my mind with the truths from His word about my worth in Christ as well as God's love and mercy for me. Doing so has enabled me to no longer cower before Satan's taunts.

- What about you? What verse do you rely on to shut the mouth of the Shamer?

10. In Psalm 25:21 (The Message), David summarizes sanctification as follows:

> *Use all your skill to put me together;*
> *I wait to see your finished product.*

- What things about you have you enjoyed waving bye-bye to as He works in you? What in the finished product will you be glad to see finally gone? What do you most look forward to seeing in it?

Jehovah Mekoddishkem & You

———◆•◆———

1. Who is *Jehovah Mekoddishkem* in your own words?

2. How has acknowledging *Jehovah Mekoddishkem* as your personal Sanctifier impacted your life?

3. Take some time to write a prayer, poem or Thank You letter to *Jehovah Mekoddishkem*.

4. **God Hunt:** Treat yourself to a *Jehovah Mekoddishkem* Hunt. Look for signs of His presence in Scripture, in nature, in hymns, in others, in the mirror. Invite Him to do His great work in you, shaping you into the masterpiece He created you to be. Record how you have surrendered to His Master design and have seen His perfecting work in you during the week.

I saw *Jehovah Mekoddishkem* _____

_____

_____

Date _____

I saw *Jehovah Mekoddishkem* _____

_____

_____

Date _____

I saw *Jehovah Mekoddishkem* _____

_____

_____

Date _____

5. **A Songfest to *Jehovah Mekoddishkem*:** Music can move words of truth from our heads to our hearts. Here are a few songs that highlight *Jehovah Mekoddishkem*. Add your favorites and then grab your instrument of choice or perhaps sing along with a CD or a YouTube video on the Internet. Make a joyful noise to *Jehovah Mekoddishkem*!

Ten Thousand Reasons
Every Moment of Every Day
I Know Whom I Have Believed
Take Time to Be Holy
Change My Heart, O Lord
Breathe on Me, Breath of God

Add any of your favorites:

_____

_____

Notes:

"Now unto the King eternal, immortal, invisible, the only wise God, be honour and glory for ever and ever. Amen."

I Timothy 1:17 KJV

18

El Olam

THE EVERLASTING GOD

*The God Who Replaces Our
Dead Ends with Life*

BASIC FACTS

- The Hebrew word *El* means "mighty" or "strong"; the word *Olam* refers to everlasting time or space. Together they translate as "the Everlasting God."
- The Hebrew name is first used in Genesis, where Abraham calls on *El Olam*.
- The name is also used in Isaiah, where the prophet exalts the Everlasting One while rebuking the Israelites' lack of faith.
- Moses references the same Everlasting God many times throughout the Old Testament.
- Humanity can have the everlastingness of God in and through Jesus Christ.

EL OLAM IN THE BIBLE

1. Having made a treaty with his potentially hostile neighbors, Abraham planted a tree to memorialize God's eternal presence with him every step of the way.

- Read Genesis 21:33. Who did Abraham call on?

- Abraham trusted *El Olam* in everything he did, especially when God asked him to sacrifice his long-awaited son Isaac. How does God's everlastingness impact your ability to cope with tests and trials?

2. Elisabeth Elliot Gren often quoted from Deuteronomy on her radio broadcast, "Gateway to Joy."

- Read her oft-quoted verse, Deuteronomy 33:27a. What adjective does Moses use to describe God? What does he say about His arms?

- How have you been buoyed by God's everlasting arms?

In chapter 8 of this Bible Study, we read about Moses holding up the staff to aid Joshua in battle. Moses' arms grew tired and he needed help.

- Read and comment on Isaiah 40:28. How does *El Olam's* endurance compare with ours?

3. Because God is eternal, all of His qualities and attributes are

also eternal. He is the same yesterday, today and forever.

- In Psalm 100:5, what three attributes of God are praised?

- I call Jeremiah 31:3b *El Olam's* love song to the Israelites and to us. Put your name in the verse as you read. Make a note here of the everlasting quality mentioned.

4. When God created us in His image, He meant for us to enjoy everlastingness with Him. But our sin nature and sinful deeds changed all that. Romans 6:23a says, *"For the wages of sin is death . . . ."* (NASB) Yet in His love, *El Olam* offers a gift to replace our dead end with life.

- Read the second part of Romans 6:23. What is the gift?

- The well-known John 3:16 reveals how each one of us can receive that gift. Read the verse (unless you have it memorized) and write out what God did to purchase the gift as well as what we must do to receive it.

- Jesus explained the source of eternal life to Martha as they stood outside the tomb of her brother Lazarus. What did Jesus say in John 11:25? Who is the source?

- Of course, the physical bodies of many who have believed in Jesus have died. In II Corinthians 5:8, Paul helps us understand what Jesus meant. Where does Paul say he (implying all believers as well) will be when he is absent from the body?

5. Do you believe what Paul says? Even so, you might not like to think about being absent from your body as you enjoy the blessings of this life. But read Psalm 90:2-6 and 12-17, a prayer of Moses.

- For how long does Moses say God is God (verse 2)?

- What do verses 5 and 6 say about the brevity of our lives?

- Comment on the New Living Testament paraphrase of verse 12: *Teach us to realize the brevity of life, so that we may grow in wisdom.* (NLT) How can that realization help you grow in wisdom?

- Apply verse 15 to your life.

6. My family was reminded of the brevity of life when my father-in-law died suddenly while visiting us. *El Olam* met our

shock with His reminder of the believer's hope in II Corinthians 4:16-5:9. Truly the knowledge of our family patriarch's immortality in Christ equipped us to cope in the temporal trial.

- Even as we look death in the eye, why do we dare not lose heart (verses 4:14 and 16)?

- What does the passage teach about our earthly tent versus our heavenly home (5:1-4)?

7. Getting up close and personal, how are you doing as your tent deteriorates in the aging process? Are you groaning like me? Surely eternal life in Christ can take the sting out of the inevitable decline, but still . . .

- I call the following verses my spiritual fountain of youth verses. To all present, past and future golden-agers, will you hang your hope on these words, as do I? Savor the words, and write your own paraphrase of the passage.

You're all I want in heaven!
You're all I want on earth!
When my skin sags and my bones get brittle,
GOD is rock-firm and faithful.
(Psalm 73:25-26 MSG)

- Isaiah 46:4 contains *El Olam's* promise to be with us in our senior years. Write the verse – maybe on a fancy note card – and save it for when you'll need it.

8. Blessed is the assurance that the Everlasting God will companion with us until we arrive safely home – until we see Him face to face. Scripture contains many promises about what heaven holds for us.

- Read I Corinthians 13:12. According to Paul, what will change when we get to heaven?

- The prophet Isaiah and the apostle John speak of other amazing changes. Read and comment on Isaiah 35:5-6 and Revelation 21:4. Which of the things mentioned do you most anticipate?

- Quoting the prophet Isaiah, Paul gives a beautiful summary of what the Everlasting God has prepared for those who love Him. Read and comment on what he says in I Corinthians 2:9.

9. As if the promise of heaven is not enough, Jesus indicates that eternal life actually begins before death.

- Read John 17:3. How does Jesus define eternal life?

- The Amplified Bible expands on the word *know* in that verse as *"to perceive, recognize, become acquainted with and understand."* What are you doing here on earth so that you may know Christ better before you meet Him in heaven?

10. The following poem fans my flame of eager enthusiasm for what awaits each believer when God replaces our earthly tent with our eternal home.

THINK OF

stepping on shore and finding it Heaven!

taking hold of a Hand and finding it God's,

breathing new air and finding it celestial,

feeling invigorated and finding it immortality,

passing from storm to an unbroken calm,

waking up and finding it HOME!

(Author Unknown)

- In Christ, aging and death are not dead ends; *El Olam* replaces those with LIFE! Are you excited about that? Record your thoughts and feelings about what is ahead for you as a believer.

El Olam, & You

————◆•◆————

1. Who is *El Olam* in your own words?

2. How has acknowledging *El Olam* as your Everlasting God impacted your life?

3. Take some time to write a prayer, poem or Thank You letter to *El Olam*.

4. **God Hunt:** Treat yourself to an *El Olam* Hunt. Look for signs of His presence in Scripture, in nature, in hymns, in others, in the mirror. Invite Him to open your eyes to see beyond the temporal to what is eternal as you face your daily challenges. Record how you have seen Him replace your dead ends with life during the week.

I saw *El Olam* _____

_____

_____

Date _____

I saw *El Olam* _____

_____

Date _____

I saw *El Olam* _____

_____

Date _____

5. **A Songfest to *El Olam*:** Music can move words of truth from our heads to our hearts. Here are a few songs that highlight *El Olam*. Add your favorites and then grab your instrument of choice or perhaps sing along with a CD or a YouTube video on the Internet. Make a joyful noise to *El Olam*!

O God, Our Help in Ages Past
Everlasting God
Blessed Assurance
When We All Get to Heaven
Heaven is a Wonderful Place
Face to Face with Christ, My Savior

Add any of your favorites:

_____

_____

Notes:

*"For momentary, light affliction is producing
for us an eternal weight of glory
far beyond all comparison. . . ."*

II Corinthians 4:17 NASB

19

Go'el

GOD MY REDEEMER

The God Who Makes All Things
Beautiful in His Time

BASIC FACTS

- *Go'el* is a Hebrew term that comes from the word *gal'al* (to redeem), and hence means "redeemer."
- The Hebrew name *Go'el* first appears in Job, although the redemption story appears from Genesis to Revelation.
- A redeemer is someone who saves, delivers or buys back a person who is somehow enslaved, by paying a price to set the person free.
- Jesus, *Go'el* Incarnate, paid a great price to buy us back and eradicate the scars of sin and suffering.

GO'EL IN THE BIBLE

1. By faith, Job hung onto his Redeemer for dear life, in spite of – or should we say, because of – devastating loss in every area of his life.

- Read Job, chapter 1 and consider what Job lost. Take note that Job did not know the reason for his losses. But one thing he did know, and to that he held fast. What does Job say in chapter 19, verse 25?

- Yes, Job was confident that *Go'el* would not forsake him forever. Read on in chapter 19, verses 26-27. What does he say that conveys that confidence?

- Compare Job's losses in chapter 1 with his gains in chapter 42:12-17. How did the Redeemer show up for him?

- What losses have you seen *Go'el* lovingly redeem in your own life?

- For what losses are you still waiting for Him to make things beautiful?

2. So that we will not lose hope in our suffering, *Go'el* fills Scripture with promises of good times to come. One such place of promise is Joel 2:22-28.

- What would cause God's people to have hope in the midst of a locust plague and severe drought (verses 22-24)?

- Because God redeems suffering, believers are encouraged to rejoice in the midst of life's trials. What is the redemptive highlight in verse 25?

- And what does God the Redeemer promise will happen after the suffering is over (verse 28)?

3. The Old Testament book of Ruth is a redemptive story with Boaz, the kinsman-redeemer, saving Ruth and Naomi from poverty and their hopeless futures as widows.

- The first chapter of Ruth reads a lot like the first chapter of Job, filled with loss. What are Naomi's losses (1:3-5)?

- How does the Redeemer God change what could have been a loss into an unexpected gain for Naomi (1: 14-17)?

- Does Ruth's undying love give you a picture of Someone else's undying love in Naomi's life (and yours)? Explain.

- Working behind the scenes throughout is *Go'el*. Read Ruth 4:14, which contains the heart of Naomi's redemption story. Who is praised? Why?

• The God who makes all things beautiful in His time turned Naomi's bitterness over her loss into joy over grandma-hood, and eventually great-grandma-hood to a king. Not just any king, mind you. Which king (Ruth 4:17)? And from that ancestry came which other King (Matthew 1:1-16; Luke 3:23-38)?

4. Boaz in the book of Ruth was a pre-figure of Jesus, who saves us from our spiritual poverty and hopeless futures as sinners. As Boaz redeemed Naomi and Ruth, so Jesus – *Go'el* Incarnate – redeems us.

• In Ephesians 1:7, what is it that Paul says redeems us?

• Part of the definition for the word *redeem* is "to buy back." According to Revelation 5:9, for whom did Christ buy us?

5. In a way, Jesus is not just a Redeemer but also a Kinsman – a blood relative of ours. His blood paid the purchase price for our redemption, allowing our entrance into the family of God when we receive Him (John 1:12). As our Kinsman, He can relate to what we go through.

• According to Hebrews 4:14-15, how can we know that our Kinsman-Redeemer understands our suffering?

(Read the wonderful wording in The Message if you can.)

- Tell about a time when you felt alone in your suffering but gained comfort in knowing that Jesus understood.

6. In Christ no suffering is wasted. This truth became real to me when, after a week of telling my redemption story to an auditorium of families touched by disability, I received a plaque engraved with Isaiah 43:1b.

- Read and write out the verse.

For me, those words proved that my life with no legs was not just worth it for me, but of great benefit to others. God had taken what I had considered an ugly deformity and made it beautiful in His time.

- What is currently the hardest trial in your life? Describe how you can hand over its ugliness to *Go'el* so He can open your eyes to see its beauty. (Listen closely – you may hear Him call your name!)

- The following rendition of Isaiah 43:1-4 from The Message puts my verse in context. What words or phrases thrill your heart with the extent of God's love toward you, a love so intense that He would die for you?

> *But now, GOD's Message, the God who made*
> *you in the first place, Jacob, the One who got*
> *you started, Israel: "Don't be afraid, I've re-*
> *deemed you. I've called your name. You're*
> *mine. When you're in over your head, I'll be*
> *there with you. When you're in rough waters,*
> *you will not go down. When you're between*
> *a rock and a hard place, it won't be a dead*
> *end — because I am GOD, your personal God,*
> *The Holy of Israel, your Savior. I paid a huge*
> *price for you: all of Egypt, with rich Cush and*
> *Seba thrown in! That's how much you mean*
> *to me! That's how much I love you! I'd sell off*
> *the whole world to get you back, trade the*
> *creation just for you."* (Isaiah 43:1-4 MSG)

7. *Go'el's* promise to redeem the suffering in our lives overflows in the Isaiah 61:3.

- Read the verse and write down the three couplets depicting the worst in our lives being replaced by God's best.

  _____instead of _____

  _____instead of _____

  _____instead of _____

- Use the three-couplet pattern to give examples of God's

redemptive work in your own life.

_____instead of _____

_____instead of _____

_____instead of _____

- Is there an area of suffering in which you are still waiting for His redemption? Write a short description of it here. Now imagine *Go'el* spraying gold over it, just as my dad sprayed gold paint over the orthopedic shoe from the stilts I wore as a child. If you have gold glitter, sprinkle it over the description you just wrote as a reminder!

8. As was true with the Israelites in Bible times, our suffering sometimes can be a result of our own disobedience and failure. Helen Carter's notable quotable includes a truth that I heard her repeat in a weekly Bible study 30 years ago. (I've preserved it in the margin of my Bible.)

> Every time you fail I have a redemptive plan.
> If you will give me all that you've got – all your
> inadequacies and failed resolutions – and come
> to me in believing faith, I will give you all that
> I have. Love Go'el, Your Redeeming God

- What haunting failure do you need to hand over to your Redeemer God in believing faith?

• What does He promise to give you in exchange?

9. As if replacing our painful experiences with beauty isn't enough, *Go'el* has given us WOW promises that make our suffering eternally worthwhile.

• Read II Corinthians 4:17 in as many translations as you have available. What do our troubles achieve for us?

• What reward does God promise in James 1:12 to those who persevere in their suffering?

10. How comforting to know that our suffering is temporary and our greatest glory is yet to come!

• Read Isaiah 35:10 and write out this triumphant verse. Yes, in Christ there is a happy ending!

I love the Message version and picture *Go'el* leading the march.

> *The people* GOD *has ransomed will come back on this road. They'll sing as they make their way home to Zion, unfading halos of joy encircling their heads, welcomed home with gifts of joy and gladness as all sorrows and*

sighs scurry into the night.
(Isaiah 35:10 MSG)

- Are you ready to take your place in *Go'el's* redemption parade? What song are you singing on the way Home? What sorrows will you see scurrying into the night?

Go'el & You

1. Who is *Go'el* in your own words?

2. How has acknowledging *Go'el* as your personal Redeemer impacted your life?

3. Take some time to write a prayer, poem or Thank You letter to *Go'el*.

4. **God Hunt:** Treat yourself to a *Go'el* Hunt. Look for signs of His presence in Scripture, in nature, in hymns, in others, in the mirror. Invite Him to open your eyes to see how great the price He paid in redeeming you. Record how you have seen Him turning this week's trials into something beautiful.

I saw *Go'el* _____

_____

_____

Date _____

I saw *Go'el* _____

_____

_____

Date _____

I saw *Go'el* _____
_____
_____
Date _____

5. **A Songfest to *Go'el*:** Music can move words of truth from our heads to our hearts. Here are a few songs that highlight *Go'el*. Add your favorites and then grab your instrument of choice or perhaps sing along with a CD or a YouTube video on the Internet. Make a joyful noise to *Go'el*!

Something Beautiful
There is a Redeemer
Unredeemed
I Know That My Redeemer Liveth
I Will Sing of My Redeemer
Redeemed (How I Love to Proclaim It)

Add any of your favorites:

_____
_____

Notes:

"Keep your eyes open for GOD,
watch for his works, be alert for signs
of his presence."

Psalm 105:4 MSG

20

A Review

LIVING DAILY IN
THE NAMES OF GOD

Congratulations on completing the *Living in the Names of God Bible Study*! Hopefully you are recognizing God's variegated presence throughout the week in the world around you, in secular as well as spiritual settings, in relationships, in music, in Scripture.

God's attribute of omnipresence means He is on the scene on every page of the Bible, on every page of history and every page of our lives whether we see Him or not. *Elohim* walked and talked with Adam and Eve in the Garden of Eden. He intercepted Father Abraham's world as *El Elyon, Adonai, El Shaddai, El Olam* and *Jehovah Jireh*. Hagar was comforted by *El Roi*; Moses was strengthened by encounters with *Jehovah, Jehovah Rapha, Jehovah Nissi, Jehovah Mekoddishkem* and *Adonai Tsuri*; Gideon was emboldened by *Jehovah Shalom*. Job's faith was empowered by the presence of *Go'el*. The shepherd boy David basked in an intimate relationship with *Jehovah Raah*. Isaiah was humbled after meeting *El Gibbor*; Jeremiah was encouraged by *Jehovah Tsidkenu*; and Ezekiel was buoyed by *Jehovah Shammah*.

Psalm 23 provides a great review for many of the Hebrew

names we've studied. Use the Names of God Reference Guide
(page vii) and apply what you've learned by filling in the blanks.

PSALM 23 (KJV)

Verse	Implied Name of God
The Lord is my Shepherd	_____
I shall not want	_____
He maketh me to lie down in green pastures. He leadeth me beside still waters.	_____
He restoreth my soul	_____
He leadeth me in paths of righteousness.	_____
Yea, though I walk through the valley of the shadow of death I will fear no evil	_____
For Thou art with me.	_____
Thou preparest a table before me in the presence of mine enemies	_____
And I will dwell in the house of the LORD forever.	_____

One thousand years after David wrote Psalm 23, Immanuel – God with us – entered time. The Son of God came to earth embodying all of the Old Testament Hebrew names. The goal of this Bible Study is to equip you to detect His presence and His power. We will each react differently. . . . The goal is for us to react in some way. As I sense His Person intercepting my life, I shout from the rooftops, "I saw Jesus today!" Pastor Don Needham is more subtle, journaling about yet another God Marker in his life. Mia Moreing Russell draws a picture depicting the Hebrew name of God that touched her world. Armida Snyder composes a poem.

What about you? How do you (or how do you plan to) track your God sightings?

In closing, my prayer for you comes from David's words in the Old Testament quoted by the apostle Peter in the book of Acts. May these words become your heart-song as you become increasingly aware of our God, whose bigness requires oh-so-many names, showing up big time in your life.

> *I saw God before me for all time. Nothing can shake me; he's right by my side. I'm glad from the inside out, ecstatic; I've pitched my tent in the land of hope. I know you'll never dump me in Hades; I'll never even smell the stench of death. You've got my feet on the life-path, with your face shining sun-joy all around.* (Acts 2:25-28 MSG)

Notes:

_____

_____

_____

_____

_____

_____

_____

_____

_____

_____

_____

_____

_____

_____

_____

_____

_____

_____

_____

_____

_____

_____

_____

_____

_____

End Notes

1   Taken from Bob Bonner's sermon: The Secret:
    Psalm 46, September 9, 1997.

2   Ligonier Blog, http://www.ligonier.org/blog/what-does-coram-
    deo-mean (accessed January 11, 2014).

3   J.I. Packer, *Knowing God* (Downers Grove: Inter-Varsity Press,
    1973), 29.

4   *The Names of God Bible*, General Editor: Ann Spangler (Baker-
    Publishing Group, 2011), 10.

5   Henrietta C. Mears, *What the Bible Is All About* (USA: Gospel
    Light Publications, 1966), 623.

6   *Sitting by My Laughing Fire*, by Ruth Bell Graham, Copyright
    © 1977 The Ruth Graham Literary Trust, used by permission,
    All rights reserved.

7   Oswald Chambers, *My Utmost for His Highest* (New York:
    Dodd, Mead & Company, 1966).

8   Phillip Keller, *A Shepherd Looks at Psalm 23* (Grand Rapids:
    Zondervan, 2007).

9   Susan Schoenian, "Sheep 201: A Beginner's Guide to Raising
    Sheep," Sheep 101, http://www.sheep101.info/201/about.html
    (accessed 23 January, 2014).

10 Henrietta C. Mears, Op. cit., p. 215.

11 Corrie ten Boom, *Tramp for the Lord* (New Jersey: Fleming H.
    Revell Company, 1974), 55.

12 Nathan Stone, *Names of God* (Chicago: The Moody Bible Insti-
    tute of Chicago, 1944), 87.

13 Max Lucado, *Life Lessons with Max Lucado: Book of James* (Nashville: Nelson Impact, 2006), 36.

14 Nathan Stone, Op. cit., p. 34.

15 Ibid., p. 34.

16 Taken from Bob Bonner's sermon: The Pursuit of God: Judges 6:1-24, August 28, 2011.

17 Matthew Henry, "Matthew Henry's Complete Bible Commentary Online," http://www.biblestudytools.com/commentaries/matthew-henry-complete/exodus/17 (accessed 4 February, 2014).

18 Brennan Manning, *The Ragamuffin Gospel* (Sisters, Oregon: Multnomah Publishers, Inc., 2000), 98.

19 R.C. Sproul, *The Holiness of God* (Wheaton, Illinois: Tyndale House Publishers, Inc., 1985), 40.

20 Taken from Ray Stedman's sermon: If God Be for Us, Romans 8:29-39 in the series From Guilt to Glory – Explained, November 7, 1976.

RECOMMENDED BOOKS
FOR NAMES OF GOD

Lord, I Want to Know You
by Kay Arthur

The Peace and Power of Knowing God's Name
by Kay Arthur

Teacups Full of Treasures:
Let the Names of God Be Your Source of Strength
by Mary Grace Birkhead

The Names of God by Ken Hemphill

The Names of God by Marilyn Hickey

All the Divine Names and Titles in the Bible
by Herbert Lockyer

Intimate Moments with the Hebrew Names of God
by Barri Cae Mallin and Shmuel Wolkenfeld,

The Names of God by Ann Spangler

The Names of God Bible edited by Ann Spangler

Living in the Names of God by Judy Squier

Names of God by Nathan Stone

The Names of God by Lester Sumrall

The Names of God pamphlet by Rose Publishing

My Father's Names by Elmer L. Towns

About the Author

Judy Squier

Born without legs, Judy lived her childhood years in the Chicago-land Area. She graduated from the University of Illinois with a Masters Degree in Speech Pathology, then moved to the San Francisco Bay Area where she and husband David resided for forty years. They've now retired to southern Oregon, and their lives are blessed by three amazing daughters, their hubbies plus an ever-growing number of grandchildren.

Judy is a former speech pathologist, a public speaker, a freelance writer and the published author of three books: *His Majesty in Brokenness*, *Living in the Names of God* and now a *Living in the Names of God Bible Study*. Ever present in her books is the message that the Christian life is at its best when a believer's theology becomes autobiography.

Judy has been an inspirational speaker since age thirteen and is available for speaking engagements worldwide.

Learn More:
WWW.JUDYSQUIER.COM

About the Artist

Mia Moreing Russell

A native Californian, raised in the San Francisco Bay Area, Mia is a retired salon owner & stylist, who soon discovered a passion for sketching and painting. Inspired by her faith in Jesus Christ, Mia uses a variety of mediums and is motivated by the beauty found in God's creation, His Word and in the texture, color and composition found in His handiwork.

Mia is married to her husband Bob of 27 years and has two grown daughters who live in the San Francisco Bay Area. Bob and Mia reside in Redwood City, CA along with their 13 year old Rat Terrier, Lucy.

Mia and Judy connected when Mia began sending Judy artwork for each name of God, while reading the *Living in the Names of God* chapter book. Thank you, Mia, for granting permission for your art to be used throughout this Bible Study.

Learn More:
www.MiaRussellArtist.com

ALSO BY JUDY SQUIER

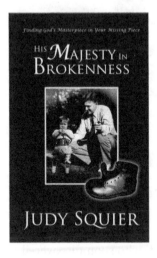

HIS MAJESTY IN BROKENNESS

Big or small, missing pieces can break the best of us. Who doesn't want to escape life's brokenness that weakens and disables us? Or does it? Unable to run from her birth defect, Judy's life became a stage for God to show up and craft a masterpiece out of her detested missing pieces. Be fortified and set free as you encounter Judy's authentic responses to daily struggles. May you, like she, discover the One who makes suffering worth all the pain.

LIVING IN THE NAMES OF GOD

Judy, born without legs, was an Average Joe Christian until an accident knocked her off of her feet. Her SOS cry was answered by *El Shaddai* and others of His Hebrew names beginning a life-transforming love relationship with the God who longs to be our All in All. True life begins when human need sends out an SOS and the human heart says yes to God's offer: "I'm here for you. I promise to bring you through. May I?"

Available at:
WWW.JUDYSQUIER.COM